D0550242

THE BEDFORDSHIRE
HISTORICAL RECORD
SOCIETY

Printed and Typeset by Advance Offset (Hitchin) Ltd.

THE PUBLICATIONS OF THE BEDFORDSHIRE
HISTORICAL RECORD SOCIETY
VOLUME 61

Law and Order in Georgian Bedfordshire

by
ERIC STOCKDALE

PUBLISHED BY THE SOCIETY   1982

CONTENTS

ACKNOWLEDGEMENTS

Once again it gives me great pleasure to acknowledge my indebtedness for help received from Miss Patricia Bell and her staff at the County Record Office. Thanks are also due to the staffs of the British Library, Public Record Office, and the London Library. I am also grateful to Mr. William St. Clair, the owner of Philip Hunt's letters, and to my wife, Joan Stockdale, for all her help.

ABBREVIATIONS

Documents referred to in the footnotes are in the Bedfordshire County Record Office unless another repository is named.

B.H.R.S. Bedfordshire Historical Record Society.
B.L. British Library
P.R.O. Public Record Office.

SALIENT DATES

1756	Seven Years' War begins; John Howard a prisoner in France.
1757	Militia Act; Bedfordshire militia riots.
1760	Bedfordshire militia embodied to repel invasion; George III succeeds George II.
1763	Duke of Bedford negotiates peace treaty; end of Seven Years' War.
1773	John Howard appointed High Sheriff of Bedfordshire.
1775	The American colonies revolt; transportation to America ceases.
1776	The Hulks Act passed by Parliament.
1777	John Howard's *The State of the Prisons* published.
1778	France signs treaty of alliance with Americans; militia embodied for second time.
1787	First convicts transported to New South Wales.
1789	French revolution.
1793	War with France again; militia embodied for third time.
1799	Philip Hunt inducted as Rector of St. Peter's, Bedford, but sails for Constantinople with the Earl of Elgin.
1801	Hunt helps to dismantle the Parthenon for Elgin.
1803	Hunt a prisoner in France.
1806	Hunt in Ireland with the Duke of Bedford.
1809	Appeal to Samuel Whitbread from the hulks; Whitbread's militia 'riot'.
1815	Hunt begins his twenty year period as visiting justice to Bedford prison; war with France ends; death of Whitbread.
1818	Hunt recommends new penitentiary at Bedford.
1820	George IV succeeds George III.
1827	Hunt gives evidence to Lord John Russell's Select Committee on Criminal Commitments and Convictions.
1829	Metropolitan Police established.
1830	William IV succeeds George IV.
1835	Bedford borough police established.
1837	Victoria succeeds William IV.
1838	Death of Hunt.
1840	County police established.

INTRODUCTION

No full study of the problems of law and order in Georgian times in Bedfordshire has yet appeared, and the writer hastens to add that he makes no claim
that the present work amounts to such a study. Rather, it is a collection of
five essays touching on some of the matters which such a study would have to
consider in depth. The explanation for the present limited work goes back to
1977, when the Bedfordshire Historical Record Society (jointly with
Phillimore & Co. Ltd.) published the writer's *A Study of Bedford Prison
1660-1877*. During the course of his research for that work the writer came
across many interesting incidents and characters connected with the prison,
or involved with other links in the law and order chain which has prison as its
final, or penultimate link. He was obliged to resist the temptation to pursue
every single item which interested him, but he resolved to follow up some of
the more fascinating ones in due course. The essays contained in the present
volume are a part of the result of that follow-up and may accordingly be
regarded in the nature of an appendix to the prison history. Three other
essays by the writer on allied topics have already appeared elsewhere, and
may be of interest to the reader concerned with the history of the prison and
the lives of those involved with it.

   The first was a biographical sketch of Sir John Kelyng, which was included
in the Society's miscellaneous volume in 1980.[1] Kelyng, who presided at
John Bunyan's trial in Bedford in January 1661, turned out on a fuller investigation to have been even more odious than one had suspected. Bunyan had
given a vivid thumbnail sketch of his own judge in *Pilgrim's Progress* when he
portrayed Lord Hategood presiding at the trial of Faithful. Kelyng's behaviour at Bunyan's trial was typical of the man, who bullied prisoners and
others throughout his career. He died in 1671 whilst Bunyan was still in
custody, and according to Lord Campbell, a later Chief Justice and Lord
Chancellor, 'he expired, to the great relief of all who had any regard for the
due administration of justice'. Strong words, but amply justified. Unfortunately Bunyan did not live to read them.

   One of the great events in penal history was the appointment of John
Howard as High Sheriff of Bedfordshire in 1773. As is well known, Howard
was so appalled by the conditions in Bedford prison that he travelled extensively in Britain, and then in the rest of Europe, to see how other authorities
coped — or failed to cope — with the universal problems entailed in confining
men against their will. In 1777 his great work *The State of the Prisons* ap-

peared — the first major study of its kind. In 1977 the writer was invited to help to organise and to speak at an international conference organised by the Howard League for Penal Reform at Canterbury to celebrate the bicentenary of the publication of Howard's internationally acknowledged book. The writer there discussed the influence of his neighbours on Howard, and made the point 'that Bedford prison itself, and the local community's interest in it, formed a part of Howard's background which should not be overlooked when one considers what may have spurred the great man on to undertake the journeys which led to *The State of the Prisons* being published in 1777'.[2]

The third essay arising from the research which has already appeared in print was about the fraught relationship of the first Inspectors of Prisons, appointed by Lord John Russell when Home Secretary, with Joshua Jebb who became the first Surveyor-General of Prisons. The writer stumbled on this story of conflict when looking in London for documents relating to Bedford prison, and when he married up the relevant Home Office papers in the Public Record Office with Jebb's correspondence in the library of the London School of Economics, a few hundred yards away. The principal protagonists were all concerned with the prison at Bedford, but their bickering ranged over many other issues.[3]

The present five essays all have a similar background in that they arose out of the research into the prison and local crime, and the people involved, whether as offenders, constables, jailers or magistrates. The essays have a common law and order background, but they also have other features in common. Each of them may be said to have a background of war, or to have features attributable to war or to post-war distress. Each is concerned in different ways with power: its use and abuse. That is perhaps scarcely surprising, as the whole concept of law and order is bound up with the application of lawful power with a view to upholding law and order, to restoring it should it break down, and to the punishment of those guilty of breaking the law. What is interesting is to see how some men will use power with discretion, whilst others will be less wise. We shall see Lord Hardwicke as an example of the former, and John, 4th Duke of Bedford as an example of the latter. We shall see Samuel Whitbread the Younger vacillating between the two schools, but coming down essentially in favour of the former. We shall also see how the extent of men's compassion, or lack of it, can be judged from their actions, speeches and letters many years later.

The first of the present essays is concerned with the Bedfordshire militia riots of 1757 — probably the most serious occasion ever of a breakdown of law and order in the county.[4] The riots occurred mainly because of the fears, not wholly unjustified, that militiamen might be required to serve overseas. The controversial Militia Act of 1757, which had been steered through the House of Commons by Thomas Potter of Ridgmont, was passed because of the danger of invasion by the French, the Seven Years' War having started in the previous year. The war was to continue until the successful conclusion of the peace negotiations conducted in 1763 by the Duke of Bedford, supported by the Earl of Bute (of Luton Hoo). The terms of the peace were extremely unpopular because they were thought to be too favourable to the defeated enemy, and this fact was partly responsible for the unpopularity of the Duke, and also for his suffering at the hands of the mobs more than any other contemporary statesman. The Member of Parliament for nearby Aylesbury, who had entered the House of Commons for the first time a few weeks before the riots of 1757 with Thomas Potter's help, expressed his disgust with a much-quoted jibe. Bedford's peace was 'like the peace of God, for it passeth all understanding', said John Wilkes, soon to be the cause of rioting in England and America.

There was nothing unusual about there being a riot in Georgian times: there were riots brought about by all sorts of grievances, and by tumultuous support for popular personalities such as Wilkes. What was unusual about the 1757 riots was that the government seemed to accept that law and order could not wholly triumph. The local constables were useless when it came to dealing with the riots. Although troops could ensure that there was no further rioting, provided they were available at the right time and place, they could not ensure a compliance with the Militia Act. We shall see how Lord Hardwicke, the recently retired Lord Chancellor, had some very sage remarks to make about the enforcement of an unpopular law which was opposed by many people all over the country. Although out of office he had considerable influence with the government, in which one of his sons served as Solicitor-General, and his son-in-law, Lord Anson, as First Lord of the Admiralty. We shall be more concerned with the son who lived at Wrest, Lord Royston. The power of the State was challenged by the rioters, who succeeded in two ways. First, the Act was allowed for all practical purposes to lapse for a few years. Secondly, it would seem that none of the Bedfordshire rioters were punished for their participation in the disorders. There were many people involved in the riots, but that factor does not usually lead to a total failure to prosecute any of the rioters concerned. Some offenders are usually apprehended and tried, but on this occasion a Nelsonian blind eye appears to have been turned not only by the local constables, but also by the government itself despite the fact that the Lord Lieutenant of the county, the Duke of Bedford, was all for firmness at all material times.

The ending of the Seven Years' War had wide-ranging effects. 'The very success of the war carried with it the germs of disintegration of the British Empire in North America,' Eric Robson pointed out. 'Victory removed the most powerful practical restraint upon the growth of separation — the presence of the hostile French in Canada on the flank of the colonists — and gave free play to the tendency to separation.'[5] The separation, when it occurred, affected many convicts in Britain. Some American colonists were unenthusiastic about receiving the many felons who were transported to Virginia and Maryland before the revolution, although others welcomed them as cheap labour. Benjamin Franklin (whose favourite author was Bunyan) had earlier made an ironic suggestion. He suggested that American rattlesnakes should no longer be killed by his compatriots. 'I would humbly propose that this general sentence of death be changed for transportation. . . . Some thousands might be collected annually and transported to Britain. There I would propose to have them carefully distributed . . . but particularly in the gardens of the prime ministers, the lords of trade, and members of Parliament, for to them we are most particularly obliged.'[6]

One of the first results of the American revolution in 1775 was that Franklin and his colleagues saw to it that convicts could no longer be sent across the Atlantic — and that no rattlesnakes were sent in the opposite direction! In 1776 Parliament passed the Hulks Act as a temporary measure to deal with the convicts stranded — with mixed feelings, no doubt — in this country. Prisoners were to be kept in the hulks of old ships and put to work on the Thames instead of in the fields of Virginia and Maryland.

'We should certainly be justified in saying that Great Britain bestowed upon America a total of 30,000 felons during the eighteenth century,' A. E. Smith, the authority on early transportation, concluded.[7] Needless to say, with large numbers involved there were not enough hulks available immediately to accommodate all those who would otherwise have crossed the Atlantic, so prisoners accumulated in prisons like Bedford in intolerable conditions — not unlike those of today, when Bedford prison can make the dubious claim to fame of being the most overcrowded of all our prisons. The parallel was referred to recently in a House of Commons debate on prisons by the Rt. Hon. Peter Archer, Q.C., M.P., the Opposition Front Bench spokesman on legal matters. Perhaps the writer may be forgiven the immodesty involved in a quotation from *Hansard.* Mr Archer said: 'It has been said many times that the problems are not new. No one pretends that they crept up on us. My hon. Friend the Member for Wolverhampton, North-East (Mrs. Short) mentioned some words of John Howard in 1777. I am indebted to Judge Stockdale's excellent book on Bedford prison for a quotation from a communication addressed by the justices of Bedford to the Government in 1783. They said:

"The keepers of the jails and bridewell of this County, having complained to the court that the said prisons are very much crowded by felons convicted at the different Assizes still remaining there, and the said complaint upon enquiry appearing to be well founded, it is ordered by this court that the right Honourable Frederick Lord North, one of his Majesty's principal Secretaries of State, be acquainted with the said complaint, in hopes that some method may be thought of for removing of the said convicts, which if not done, by more prisoners being from time to time committed to the said prisons . . . these will be rendered unhealthy and the consequences may be fatal not only to the persons confined in the said prisons, but also to the inhabitants of the Town of Bedford."

'The Home Secretary at the time had an answer. He said that he would send the prisoners to the hulks and that in due course they would be dispatched to America or to Botany Bay. That is an option which is no longer open to the prison authorities. But the Bedford justices pinpointed a problem which has been with us ever since. The reason for the desperation being felt within the prison service is that the prison authorities do not control the number of people committed to their custody. Local prisons learn at the end of each day how many people have been dispatched there by the courts when the prisoners arrive at reception. No one inquires whether there is room. The prisoners are there and the authorities must find room.'[8]

It was not until 1786 that Botany Bay was chosen as a substitute destination, and it was May 1787 before the First Fleet sailed for Australia with a cargo of convicts. Two years later the first prisoners from Bedford set sail for the new continent. The squalor on board the hulks where many of them were kept before their departure can be imagined. One has only to imagine the old Bedford prison being dumped in the middle of the River Ouse to get some idea. (Come to think of it, that is precisely what did happen to the minute old borough prison, so often *wrongly* depicted in modern editions of Bunyan's books as the prison in which he was kept, for he was in fact in the county prison.) The third essay deals with an appeal made to Samuel Whitbread the Younger by a prisoner kept on a hulk at Woolwich, pending his departure for Botany Bay.

Samuel Whitbread was a fascinating man, whose full biography has not yet been written. Roger Fulford produced an entertaining volume on the Whig politician in 1967, and Alan Cirket edited his notebooks for the Society in 1971, but a mere glance at Whitbread's correspondence in the County Record Office and at reports of contemporary Parliamentary debates shows how much remains to be done.[9] Cirket quoted Whitbread's obituary in the *Northampton Mercury* which described him as 'the constant, able and disinterested advocate of justice, freedom and humanity, wherever and by whomsoever assailed. No man who had a claim on the virtuous for protection ever applied to him in vain. He was the earnest and indefatigable friend of the oppressed.' This praise was undoubtedly justified, yet Whitbread was a complex mixture. We shall see what his friend Thomas Creevey had to say of him after a stay at Southill. Whilst one of the most bitter opponents of the war with France, Whitbread was a keen militia colonel in the years when an invasion by the French was once more feared, and when the militia was called on again for additional protection. Whitbread's ill-advised conduct towards his non-commissioned officers — all civilians — will be considered in the fourth essay, as will the oppressive manner in which his adjutant Charles Bailey (later to be Mayor of Bedford) tried to restore order. Bailey even clapped one of the sergeants into the borough prison — though by then, fortunately, the one in the river had been replaced by one on dry land.

The second essay deals with a remarkable clerical magistrate, Philip Hunt, who supervised the county prison for the twenty years following on the end of the Napoleonic war, when unemployment and high food prices had their effect on crime figures. The number of offenders against the game laws increased substantially, and so did the problem of prison overcrowding. Hunt's fascinating earlier history is discussed in detail, even though that entails following him to Constantinople and Athens, places he visited whilst simultaneously Rector of St. Peter's, Bedford, and secretary and chaplain to the Earl of Elgin. Hunt's vital contribution to the obtaining of the Elgin Marbles is considered. Perhaps the best justification for the lengthy discussion of Hunt's exploits is that he was one of the most interesting Bedfordshire personalities to emerge during the writer's research over a period of years — and yet he has been scarcely referred to in the literature. The war had its part in his story also. The obtaining of the marbles and other antiquities was speeded up partly because of the fear that the French might get to them first; and it was facilitated because the Turks, who occupied Greece, were pleased with the British because of their successes against the French. It is sometimes alleged that Elgin and Hunt stole the marbles from the Greek people and that they should therefore be returned to Athens. The British government has recently announced that they will not be returned, so the results of Elgin's and Hunt's efforts may still be appreciated in the British Museum in the future.[10] Incidentally, if the marbles were stolen, then presumably Hunt was guilty of a species of white-collar crime: dog-collar crime perhaps?

Whilst Hunt was on his journey home he was made prisoner by the French, just as John Howard had been in 1756. The experience of captivity must have influenced their later interests and increased their compassion for those behind bars. 'When I first was put into prison some people advised me to try and forget who I was,' wrote Oscar Wilde from Reading jail. 'It was ruinous advice. It is only by realising what I am that I have found comfort of any kind. Now I am advised by others to try on my release to forget that I have ever been in a prison at all. I know that would be equally fatal. . . . To reject one's own experiences is to arrest one's own development.'[11] Whilst neither Howard nor Hunt would have approved of Wilde, they would have understood him and would probably have agreed with these sentiments.

It was Hunt's experience as a magistrate and as the principal visiting justice of Bedford prison which qualified him to give evidence to a Parliamentary committee on law and order topics, but it was the sum of all his experiences which made his contributions particularly valuable. The importance of the magistracy in local affairs in Georgian times was well illustrated by Sidney and Beatrice Webb in their great English Local Government series. Both Whitbread and Hunt were good examples of the better type of responsible, caring magistrate, who tried to ensure that calls for law and order were accompanied by a degree of compassion, and by a realistic acceptance of what can, and what cannot, be achieved by the forces of law and order.

Nowadays when the expression 'law and order' is used the first institution that comes to mind is the police. Thereafter one thinks of the legal framework, the courts and punishment. In Georgian times there was, of course, no police force in the modern sense at all. The village constable tottered from crisis to crisis through his year of office, and if he was lucky there was no serious outbreak of disorder or crime on his patch during that year. With any luck, trouble would be over the boundary of his jurisdiction, or outside his term of office. In the final essay the unsatisfactory nature of the constable's impotence is discussed, as are the various measures taken to supplement his meagre powers in times of need. Help was sometimes to be found in the county: sometimes it had to be obtained from London — fortunately only a few hours away. It was in Georgian times that it became increasingly apparent that a professional police force would have to be set up, and it was near the end of the reign of George IV that the capital obtained its own force. Bedford borough and the county had to wait until the following decade, but the coming of the police may fairly be said to fall squarely within the period we are considering.

1. 'Sir John Kelyng, Chief Justice of the King's Bench 1665-1671', *B.H.R.S.* Vol. 59, (1980) p.43.
2. 'John Howard and Bedford Prison', in John Freeman (ed.), *Prisons Past and Future*, Cambridge Studies in Criminology, Vol. 41, London: Heinemann, 1978, p.15.
3. 'The Rise of Joshua Jebb, 1837-1850', *British Journal of Criminology*, Vol. 16 (1976) p.164.
4. The writer would like to acknowledge his indebtedness to Tony Hayter's, *The Army and the Crowd in Mid-Georgian England*, London: Macmillan Press, 1978. The militia generally is dealt with comprehensively by J. R. Western in *The English Militia in the Eighteenth Century*, London: Routledge and Kegan Paul, 1965.
5. Eric Robson, *The American Revolution*, London: Batchworth Press, 1955, p.1.
6. Carl Van Doren, *Benjamin Franklin*, London: Putman, 1939, p.199.
7. A.E. Smith, *Colonists in Bondage*, Chapel Hill: Univ. of N. Carolina Press, 1947, p.99.

8. Parl. Deb., House of Commons, Vol.14, col.331, 2 December 1981.
9. Roger Fulford, *Samuel Whitbread 1764-1815*, London: Macmillan, 1967; Alan F. Cirket, 'Samuel Whitbread's Notebooks, 1810-11, 1813-14,' *B.H.R.S.*, Vol.50 (1971).
10. *The Times*, 16 February 1982.
11. 'De Profundis', *Complete Works of Oscar Wilde*, London: Collins, 1966, p.916.

I
THE 1757 MILITIA RIOTS

'The nation throughout the first months of 1756 lived in abject terror of an invasion. Few troops were ready to meet such a descent, for votes cannot improvise trained officers and men, and the folly of the Administration had done its worst to discourage enlistment.' So wrote Sir John Fortescue of the early panicky days of the Seven Years' War.[1] One of the responses to the threat came from some landowners who raised local forces of their own, promising the volunteers that they would not be required to serve abroad. In practice, some of the Somerset volunteers raised by Lord Ilchester and Lord Digby were driven on board transports despite their protests, and shipped to Gibraltar. Fortescue added, 'Never was there more brutal and heartless instance of the ill-faith kept by a British Government towards the British soldier.' Another response came from the government itself, which tried to get a Militia bill through Parliament in 1756. This first attempt failed, partly because of the opposition to it in the House of Lords by the Lord Chancellor, Lord Hardwicke, who was soon to resign from office.

Lord Hardwicke and his family figure so much in the story that follows that the main members should be introduced. Philip Yorke, 1st Earl of Hardwicke lived just to the east of Bedfordshire, at Wimpole on the road to Cambridge. His oldest son, another Philip, used the courtesy title of Lord Royston and lived at Wrest, Silsoe, with his wife Jemima, Marchioness Grey. Royston was a Member of Parliament for Cambridgeshire. Another of Hardwicke's sons was Charles Yorke, the Solicitor-General, who was also to be Lord Chancellor in 1770, although he died three days after his appointment. Hardwicke and Royston were very close, the son often asking the father for advice. It is interesting to note from the existing correspondence that Royston clearly preferred the counsel of the recently retired Lord Chancellor to that of the brother who was still a member of the government as one of the law officers of the Crown.

One of the other principal characters in the present story is Thomas Potter, M.P., whose life story was chequered. In 1757 the government tried once more to get a Militia Act onto the statute book. This second attempt succeeded, thanks in part to the hard work put in on the bill in the House of Commons by Potter, as chairman of the committee of the whole House considering the bill. Potter was the son of the Archbishop of Canterbury but is remembered now less for his pious background than for his dissolute revelling as one of the so-called Medmenham monks, and as the libertine companion of John Wilkes. He is also credited with being the author of the obscene *Essay on Woman,* which was to help bring Wilkes down.[2]

In December 1756 Potter was appointed Paymaster-general of the land forces, and in the following July joint vice-treasurer of Ireland. In the July Potter, with the help of his great friend William Pitt (the Elder), enabled John Wilkes to replace him as M.P. for Aylesbury. In the general election Pitt moved to a new constituency at Bath, leaving Okehampton for Potter. Potter in turn made way at Aylesbury for Wilkes, who had the privilege of paying the considerable election expenses of all three candidates. Potter lived at Ridgmont House, Ridgmont, and was one of the Deputy Lieutenants of the county. His daughter Mariana married Malcolm Macqueen and their son Thomas Potter Macqueen, who became a well-known magistrate and one of the Members of Parliament for the county, makes a brief appearance in two of the later essays.

After the July election William Pitt became one of the Secretaries of State and a mainstay of the administration headed by the Duke of Newcastle. His friendship with Potter was close, as was confirmed by a letter which Pitt wrote to his nephew Thomas Pitt at Cambridge on 7 October 1756 about Potter's son who was going up to Emanuel. 'Mr. Potter is one of the best friends I have in the world, and nothing can oblige me more than that you would do all in your power to be of assistance and advantage to the young man.'[3]

The Militia Act of 1757 provided that men were to be chosen by lot for three years part-time service, Bedfordshire being required to raise four hundred men. Although it contained many detailed provisions it was silent on the subject of pay, and this was to be one of the causes of the riots which shortly after its enactment occurred. Possibly the principal cause was the distrust of the populace on the issue of overseas service, though the Act specifically stated, 'Neither the Act, nor any matter or things herein contained, shall be deemed or construed to extend to the giving or declaring any power for the transporting any of the militia of this Realm, or any way compelling them to march out of this Kingdom.'[4] In view of what had happened to the earlier militia men who had been shipped abroad, people felt that the government was not to be trusted on that point — a matter which Hardwicke readily understood. The Act contained a detailed timetable so that there should be no delay in raising the new line of defence against the French. The Lord Lieutenant and the Deputy Lieutenants of all counties were charged with the execution of the Act which called for the first of the essential meetings to be held on the 12 July 1757.

The actual mechanics of the Act may be illustrated by extracts from a journal kept by Luke Francklin of Great Barford, who had access to the papers of his twenty-one year old nephew, John Francklin or Franklin. Despite his youth John Franklin was one of the Deputy Lieutenants of the county.[5] The excerpts relate mainly to Barford hundred, but identical procedures were legally required in all the other hundreds of the country.

The selection process started with a warrant from the chief constable of the hundred, Nicholas Levitt, such as that addressed 'To the constables and other officers of the Parish of Great Barford'. 'By virtue of an order from His Majesty's Lieutenants of the said county you are hereby ordered and commanded to make a fair and true list in writing of all the men usually and at this time dwelling within your said parish between the age of eighteen and fifty years . . . distinguishing the numbers and names of the persons in your parish and which of the persons so returned labour under any infirmities, incapacitating them from serving as militia men and you the said officers are to affix a fair and true copy of the said list with the number of men as aforesaid upon the door of your parish church on Sunday morning the 24th. day of this instant July and you the said constables are ordered and required to meet me at the *Saracen's Head* Inn in Eaton Socon on Thursday the 28th. day following and to bring with you the aforesaid list that I may transmit the same to the Lieutenants.'

A list was duly prepared containing the names of seventy-nine men in the right age range, starting with that of Luke Francklin, but omitting that of John Franklin, who as a Deputy Lieutenant was exempt. The list included the names of two men who were lame, two who were deformed, one who was deaf, one who had a wooden leg, and one described as 'almost an idiot'. That left seventy-two who qualified for the lot from Great Barford parish alone.

On Tuesday 2 August the list was brought by the chief constable to John, 4th Duke of Bedford, the Lord Lieutenant, and his Deputy Lieutenants at the *Swan* in Bedford. The totals of this and similar lists were added up and came to 8545 eligible men in the county as a whole. As the Act called for the county to provide four hundred men only, the Lieutenants decided that one man in every twenty-one should be selected by lot. As the Barford hundred (which had Great Barford as one of its parishes) had 627 eligible men it was required to produce twenty-nine for service, each parish providing its proportion.

The Duke and his colleagues divided the county into four divisions, and arranged that the next general meetings should be on 23 August and should be attended by some of the Deputy Lieutenants in each of the four places, to hear any objections to the names included in the first lists. The four locations decided upon were Bletsoe for the Barford, Willey and Stodden hundreds; Ampthill for Redbornestoke and Flitton hundreds; Hockliffe for Manshead hundred; and finally Biggleswade for the division which was to cause most of the trouble, that made up of the Biggleswade, Clifton and Wixamtree hundreds.

On 19 August the chief constable of Barford duly sent out his second warrant to his inferior officers, giving notice of the right to object at the *Falcon* at Bletsoe on 23 August. On that date some alterations were made to the lists, and then the men listed were called forward by their parish in batches of twenty-one. Each man had to draw a paper from a box containing twenty blank pieces and one marked 'Militia man'. The few remaining men were put together with those of another parish until a further twenty-one names had been collected: this was the Duke's own idea. The seventy-two fit men from Great Barford came forward. Three batches of twenty-one each produced three militia men and left nine over. Roxton parish had twelve over and so they joined the Great Barford nine to make another panel of twenty-one. It was a Great Barford man who drew the last 'vacancy', and so that parish provided four men in all to repulse the French: Edward Bertram, William Pell, Richard Simms and John Sturgeon.

The chief constable of Barford sent out his third warrant to his officers: 'These are therefore to require and order you forthwith to give notice to every person within your said parish so chosen to serve in the said Militia personally to appear at a meeting at the sign of the *Bell* in Odell the said 12th. day of September 1757.' This meeting was intended for the enrolment of the twenty-nine losers in the lottery, each of whom was sent a similar printed calling up notice, but as we shall see, that crucial meeting was to be cancelled.

The meeting at the *Swan* on 2 August, presided over by the Duke of Bedford as Lord Lieutenant, was described in some detail by Lord Royston in a letter which he wrote from Wrest that day to his father, Lord Hardwicke, at Wimpole. Royston dealt first with the post of Lord Lieutenant of Cambridgeshire for which he was being considered, although he lived in Bedfordshire. He informed his father that if Lord Granby 'has an inclination for the Lieutenancy, I shall not contest it with him. This Militia Bill will render it an office not very acceptable but to those who love a bustle'.[6]

Royston continued: 'I went to our meeting at Bedford today, and am just returned from it; there were present our Lord Lieutenant and fifteen Deputy Lieutenants, some of all parties; Sir Humphrey Monoux, Mr. Herne (the Member for Bedford), Mr. Ongley, Colonel Lee, Lord Ossory and we did all that the Act directs to be done at the 2nd meeting; — received the lists from the high constables, settled the proportions for the several hundreds, — and subdivided ourselves for the lesser meetings. I wish I may not have drawn myself into more attendances by it, for he that says *A*, can hardly avoid saying *B*, too.

'There is a good deal of grumbling amongst the lower sort of people about the Act, though no riots have yet happened. . . . The Duke of Bedford told us that he was in hope to have received some applications for commissions and that gentlemen would have recommended their friends to be officers; that in Devonshire he did not doubt, but their quota would be soon complete as well in officers as private men. I did not perceive that the military spirit was shining here or that any of the gentlemen made a tender of his service. . . . Whatever becomes of the Bill, there will be some use in knowing authentically the number of fighting men within the kingdom.'

The Duke's reference to his success in Devonshire, where he was also Lord Lieutenant, is of interest. Perhaps the Devonians were more alarmed at the prospect of a seaborne invasion than the Bedfordians — their coastline was certainly longer! The difference between the two counties was referred to later by his supporter Richard Rigby, who wrote to the Duke on 30 May 1759, 'I instanced your Grace's conduct in Bedfordshire, where you could not get a militia, though you had succeeded in Devonshire.'[7]

The Marchioness Grey was aware of some of the discontent in the county as a result of the passing of the Act, as her letter of 28 July 1757 from Wrest to her friend Catherine Talbot showed: 'You enquired once I think what steps were to be taken about the Militia Act: pray what is done in your county? Has your Lord Lieutenant held any meetings or appointed any Deputy Lieutenants and what do your people in general or your divided gentry say to it? In this county our Governor has a mind to be active, but I am told it is with great unpopularity, and that clamour is rising very high among the common people. I never believed it could be executed, or that the trouble and the subjection would be borne. The people in England never know what they clamour for, or are satisfied with what they have. This new way of numbering them in their parishes and drawing lots for their service has struck them (I hear) as being picked out and voted to destruction to save their neighbours and that degree of public spirit does not at all suit with John's disposition.'[8]

A letter from the Marchioness's husband Lord Royston to his father on 14 August confirmed that some of the gentlemen of Bedfordshire were not all that keen on the Act either. Royston had by then been chosen for the Cambridgeshire Lieutenancy and discussed arrangements for that county with his father. 'If it will be necessary, or right for me to come up, in order to kiss his Majesty's hand immediately upon my appointment, I should like to do it the beginning of next week, before you return to Wimpole. We may settle the new list of Deputy Lieutenants by then, which ought to be done before first of September, as they must subdivide themselves after the 2nd meeting. By this means too I shall avoid the trouble of attending a meeting about the Militia in the hundred where I live which was fixed without my knowledge for the 23rd of this month. The same day is appointed all over the county. I do not find that the gentlemen in my neighbourhood are at all fond of the business, or that any of them intend to take commissions, but the Duke of Bedford is very earnest in carrying the Act into execution, as far as relates to getting the men.'[9]

Whilst the drawing of lots had gone smoothly at Bletsoe, the situation at Biggleswade was rather different. According to Luke Francklin, 'At the meeting at Biggleswade on Tuesday 23rd. August for the hundreds of Biggleswade, Wixamtree and Clifton in order to have the men drawn by lot, a mob from several of the parishes in those hundreds followed the constables to Biggleswade and threatened their lives if they offered to draw the lists, upon which the constables were so intimidated that they positively refused to draw them and the Deputy Lieutenants and justices (Sir Roger Burgoyne, Richard Astell Esq. and Colonel Lee) were obliged to adjourn the meeting and order the constables to attend again on Tuesday the 30th August at the *Sun* at Biggleswade.'

On that later date some people attended and a great mob was said to be on the way, so 'Burgoyne thought proper to withdraw and took Colonel Lee home with him'. According to Francklin, 'The crowd came from Cardington, Cople, Willington, Muggerhanger, Shefford, Sandy, Potton and several other parishes, increasing as they went along, harvest men, turnip hoers, labourers and servants leaving their work to join them, so that when they got to Biggleswade their number amounted at least to 1500, some say to 2000 men.'

One of the rioters, a gardener from Sandy, bragged: 'When we found the gentlemen were fled from the inn we followed Sir Roger home. I believe there was at least 1500 of us. Sir Roger came out to talk with us and was ordering us some liquor, but we told him we did not want his beer, but the lists of the militia men which we were resolved to have returned.' Some of the lists were found to be missing, and Burgoyne thought they must be at the *Sun*, but he handed the rest over to the rioters. The gardener's account continued, 'When we had got the lists we told him, now we would drink with him, and beer was brought by pails and tubs full. When we had drank plentifully out of mugs, bowls and our hats, we insisted on every man's being paid half a crown for his loss of time, but Sir Roger thought that too unreasonable and said it would come to more money than he had in the house. At last we agreed to five shillings for each parish and ten shillings for Sandy.' After that they marched to Astell's of Everton, where they made 'the like demand'. Then on to Parson Monoux 'for he had preached against us'. After that they broke all the windows at the *Sun* in Biggleswade, a very substantial inn, and extracted some money from the unfortunate landlord. Finally they thought of paying a visit to Squire Harvey of Ickwell, but fortunately for him, 'thought it was too late in the night and so dispersed and went to our homes'.

Sir Roger Burgoyne rushed off to Woburn Abbey to report to the Duke of Bedford, but he was not there. Burgoyne wrote a hasty, rambling letter to the Duke at 3.30 on the morning of 31 August, whilst at Woburn. It is set out in full as it contains the first detailed account of the troubles, and as it led to the dispatch of troops to Bedfordshire. 'Yesterday I went to the *Sun* at Biggleswade where I met Col. Lee at 10.00 and before we had been there a quarter of an hour two constables came to inform us that they had passed a mob in two companies one consisting of about 600 and the other of 400 men who, they were informed by some of the company, intended to march into Biggleswade (which they entered in five minutes time) and their ring-leader to break into the room where we were sitting and to cry "Murder", which was to be the signal for the mob to enter and to murder every gentleman there met. We therefore thought it our best way to return to my house immediately. Immediately after we were gone the mob arrived at the *Sun* where, having been informed that I had left the lists, precepts and tickets prepared for drawing the Militia men by lot, they demanded them of Mr. Fletcher, the master of the house who refusing to deliver them, they threatened to pull down his house and murder him immediately. Notwith-standing those threats he said he would not deliver them unless he had an order from me for so doing but gave them great quantities of ale which a little pacified them, and then they determined to march immediately to my house and to murder me and pull down the house, and set out immediately upon which two of the high constables came immediately to inform me of their resolutions, upon which I ordered them to set out some hogheads of ale, but on their arriving soon after they refused the ale and said they did not come for that purpose, but for to murder me and pull down the house, and demand the tickets which were to be drawn by lot and upon consulta-tion we thought it proper to send for them to Biggleswade, which we accordingly did, and delivered to them which they instantly destroyed, and then drank several hogheads of ale, and continuing very riotous drank dam-nation to the K—, Duke of Bedford and myself. I with my family had left the house which they being informed of they declared themselves determined to murder me if above ground, and suspecting I was gone into the village threatened to burn the whole village down if they did not find me.

'After that they demanded a shilling a day a man for their day's work: Afterwards demanded a guinea a day a man and then fell their demands for £100 to be distributed among them or they would pull down the house.

'My servant at last prevailed on them to accept of a crown or half a guinea each parish (but have not since seen my servant so cannot tell which sum he gave) but am informed that the person of each parish who received the money gave their names to my servant and the parish they belonged to.

'After having been there from 12.00 at noon till 6 in the evening, they then determined to serve Mr. Astell in the same manner which they accord-ingly did receiving of him both beer and money.

'From thence they went to Mr. Kingsley's but what mischief they did there I have not heard. And from thence to Mr. Lewis Monoux, clergyman at Sandy where I hear they broke all his windows for having endeavoured to persuade them in the morning from the riotous proceedings.

'And then determined as their last act that evening to murder Mr. Fletcher at the inn and pull down his house for having refused them the tickets in the morning. And accordingly returned to Biggleswade where they joined a great number of their companions who they had left to keep guard there, and went immediately to Fletcher's where they broke all the windows, drank a quantity of ale and did considerable damage to the amount of £50 and would have murdered him if he had not got out of the way.

'They determined afterwards to go to Mr. Palmer's and Mr. Harvey's but have not heard whether they went.

'But received an account by express at Baldock this morning at 9.00 (where I with my family was obliged last night to retreat for safety) that their determination last night was to come to the Duke of Bedford's at Woburn Abbey to murder him and pull down his house as this day but what is become of them since I have not heard.

'In the situation affairs are now neither myself or my family dare return to my own house, but shall stay at Sir Thomas Salisbury's at Offley.

'All this account I have received by information mostly from my own servants as I was obliged myself to fly for safety as Mr. Astell was obliged to do the same.

'P.S. By information from Mr. Haywood of Biggleswade a rat catcher of Ickwell has declared before three witnesses that he was determined to stab me getting into my post chaise in the *Sun* yard had not a people stood between us which prevented it.'[10]

The Duke at once wrote from Market Street to Lord Barrington, the Secretary at War. 'My servant met me two miles from this place, with the inclosed letter from Sir Roger Burgoyne, which I send by him to your Lordship that orders may be given to send troops to Biggleswade, Potton, from which part of the county the chief disorder seems to arise. I believe there is no disposition of this sort in our part of the county — I am setting out immediately for Woburn.'[11]

Barrington responded immediately, with a dispatch on 31 August to the officer commanding two troops of the Royal Regiment of Horse Guards at Uxbridge and Hillingdon. 'It having been represented by His Grace the Duke of Bedford and Sir Roger Burgoyne, that there are great riots and disturbances in the county of Bedford and that several hundred rioters have assembled and have done, and threatened to do, great mischief, and it being represented that a Military Force may be necessary to suppress the same, and to preserve the public peace: It is therefore his Majesty's pleasure that you cause the two troops of the Royal Regiment of Horseguards under your command at Uxbridge and Hillingdon to march with all possible expedition, by such route as you shall think most convenient, to Biggleswade, where, or in such other place as you shall think expedient, they are to be quartered, and be aiding and assisting to the civil magistrates, at their requisition, in suppressing any riots, or disturbances, which may happen, and in apprehending and securing the rioters, and in preserving the public peace, but not to repel force with force unless it shall be found absolutely necessary, or being thereunto required by the civil magistrates.'[12]

The final instruction to avoid force if possible was routinely included in such military orders. That prudent course had been advised by Hardwicke back in 1733 when he was Attorney-General.[13]

As soon as the Duke got back to Woburn on 1 September, he wrote to William Pitt, the Secretary of State, 'I think it my duty to apprise you for his Majesty's information, and in order that I may receive instructions how to act in an affair of this delicate nature, of a very extraordinary riot that happened on Tuesday last in the eastern division of the county, upon a meeting appointed that day at Biggleswade for choosing by lot the militia men which are to be furnished by the three hundreds of Clifton, Wixamtree and Biggleswade. The account of it I received yesterday on the road, by a letter from Sir Roger Burgoyne, one of the gentlemen acting for that division, which letter I immediately despatched to the Secretary at War, in order that troops might be forthwith sent to be aiding and assisting to the civil magistrates if necessary; but not having any opportunity of taking a copy of it, and having only read it once cursorily, I cannot possibly give you the particulars of the riot, but must refer you for that to the letter now in the Secretary at War's hand.'[14] The Duke gave a short account of what he recollected of the details and continued, 'I think it my duty to represent, for the consideration of his Majesty and those of his servants he shall please to refer it to, the dangerous consequences that may attend the taking no notice of this affair, not only towards the carrying the Militia Act into execution, but to the bad example the suffering a giddy and riotous populace to stand in opposition to an act of parliament unnoticed may have upon the rest of the kingdom.

'I must however, in justice to the rest and far the greatest part of this county, observe to you, that though the raising the militia in the manner chalked out by the present bill seems unpalatable to many, yet I have not in any part of it where I have been, observed the least disposition to riot or disloyalty.

'I must likewise observe, that the meetmg on Tuesday last for the three eastern hundreds was just a week later than those for the other hundreds of the county, which were held without any obstruction on the preceding Tuesday, and was owing to some gentlemen that had engaged to come on that day forgetting their appointment, and others not being able to be found till the day was too far advanced to finish the business. There was one thing observable then, and which seemed to point out the gentlemen then present to draw the lots immediately; and that was, the petty constables absolutely refused to draw them, as they said if they did, they should subject themselves to be knocked on the head on their return to their respective parishes.'

On 1 September the Marchioness Grey wrote to her friend Catherine Talbot again; her letter included a revealing reference to the Duke. 'This absurd Militia Bill, the produce of faction in Another Place, is now the object of clamour and misrule here. The people are all mad about it and neither do nor will understand what it means; but as our Great Man has chose to hurry things on in this county faster than in any other, and is himself perhaps the least popular man in it, and the least fit to carry on any business, they are in general discontented, and in some places have rose in mobs when their names were to be drawn. I hope the same spirit will not extend into Cambridgeshire, whither my Lord is gone to hold a meeting today nor will he I believe be so eager or so military there as the Lord Lieutenant is here.'[15]

The Marchioness's hopes for peace in Cambridgeshire were not to be fulfilled, as a letter written that very day by her husband to his father indicated. Royston wrote from the *Rose* in Cambridge, and referred to the fact that the 'evil example' of Bedfordshire had spread across the county boundary. 'There was a riot at Gamlingay last night, and the lists of that parish was taken by force from the chief constable. The man said it was dark, and he could not distinguish any of them but they threatened him hard if he did not deliver it up. The petty constables are afraid of doing their duty.'[16]

The next serious outbreak in Bedfordshire was on 6 September. By then neighbouring counties had also had their share of similar trouble. On that date William Pitt wrote to Lord Barrington, 'Having received information that large numbers of people have assembled in a riotous manner in different parts of Northamptonshire and Hertfordshire, threatening and using violence against the persons and houses of the magistrates and others employed in carrying into execution the law relating to the Militia, I am commanded to signify to your Lordship his Majesty's pleasure that, out of the six troops of the Royal Regiment of Horse Guards, commanded by Sir John Ligonier, and now quartered at Hounslow, Richmond and Kingston, you do forthwith order two troops to march with all expedition to Northampton and one troop to Newport Pagnell in Northamptonshire, and it is the King's further pleasure that your Lordship do order two other of the six troops above-mentioned

to march to Royston in Hertfordshire, or such other places in that neighbourhood as shall be most convenient for quartering the troops.'[17]

On 6 September Pitt also wrote to inform Earl Cowper that his request for
troops to deal with the Herfordshire rioters had been granted, and that the
Horse Guards were on their way.[18] These troops would have been able to
help in Bedfordshire, but the Duke of Bedford was not aware of their move-
ments when he reported the outbreak of violence which had occurred on that
same day, and when he asked for more troops.

At 2.30 on the morning of 7 September the Duke wrote to Barrington
from Woburn, 'The inclosed letter from Mr. Bullock of Sharnbrook was
brought to my house about an hour and a half ago, but as I supped abroad I
have but this moment received it. Your Lordship will see by the inclosed
account, which comes from a gentlemen I can depend upon, that 59 men of the
Royal Regiment of Horse Guards (which is all the force we have now amongst
us) are not sufficient to defend the whole county from the insolence of a
riotous rabble who flushed with the success they have met with cannot be
quieted without a more considerable force than we have at present. Having
received no positive directions for my conduct, from the Secretary of State
to whom I wrote a whole account of what had passed to the 1st instant, I
found myself obliged to appoint a meeting of the Deputy Lieutenants and
justices of the peace for this county at Bedford on Friday next in the morning, in order to consult of proper measures to preserve the peace of the
county, which now seems to be in the utmost hazard, and I fear I shall find
very few of them at Bedford, unless under the protection of a strong military
force. I must therefore desire your Lordship, that a sufficient number of
troops be immediately sent to Bedford, from whence (if necessary) they may
be detached to any other part of the county. I think I can venture to assure
you, that everything in this part of the county will go well, as an association
has been signed by many the most considerable inhabitants of this hundred
(the largest in the county) for the preserving the peace of it, under the
authority of the civil magistrates.'[19]

Bullock's letter, undated but apparently written on 6 September, told an
alarming story. 'About 9 this morning I received certain intelligence, that five
or six hundred men were coming to fire my house, for which purpose they
would bring straw with them and others reported they came for the lists —
upon which I rose and saw from about half a mile off, and having sent Mrs.
Bullock (whose condition alarmed me) and the little family out of the way,
I waited in my Hall to receive them, I hope with that firmness which becomes
a man who is conscious he has been doing his duty. In a short time they came
to the gates of the forecourt upon which I went to them and asked what they
wanted. They replied, the lists of their several parishes, and a discharge for
every man who had been chosen. I had nothing to attempt but remon-

strances, which I made in the best manner I was able upon every point I could suggest, and read over the printed abstracts of each; all would avail nothing, the constables called them to silence or I had not been heard, but the moment I had done they replied it signified nothing, that they came for their lists and a discharge and they would have them. I then fetched out the lists of the returns and delivered them as they called for them, some to the officers and some to the common men; they would have a discharge on the back of their warrant and also on the back of their lists for the whole parish. I desired the officers to give me a form of what they demanded and I would sign it, after some consultation they told me I was the fittest person and they expected it from me; accordingly I did it in the shortest manner. They continued here to the numbers of near a thousand till after three.' Bullock added two warnings. 'By many accounts I hear you threatened with destruction to your person and your house to be fired or levelled to the ground. . . . They declared to my servant they will come to Bedford on Friday in a body of five or six thousand.'

According to Luke Francklin's notes about that day, 'The mob rose in Stodden and Willey hundreds and I believe from Ravensden, Goldington and Renhold in Barford hundred, but chiefly in Stodden hundred.'[20]

Bedford's letter to Barrington was answered on 7 September by the latter's Under-Secretary, Thomas Tyrwhitt, who had at once sent orders for troops to march to Bedford in time for the proposed meeting on Friday the 9th. 'In the absence of Lord Barrington I had the honour of your Grace's letter and accordingly I have sent an order to the commanding officer of the Royal Regiment of Dragoons at Romford to march two troops to Bedford, so as to be there on Friday morning. I enclose a copy of the order by which you will see that these troops are to be at the disposal of your Grace, and the civil magistrates, and may be stationed wherever you think they will be most wanted. At the same time I must inform your Grace that, by direction of Mr. Secretary Pitt, orders were sent very early this morning for the march of five troops of the Royal Regiment of Horse Guards, viz. two to Northampton, one to Newport Pagnell, and two to Royston and the parts adjacent. These troops have all orders to assist the civil magistrates, at their requisition, in suppressing riots and therefore as none of their quarters are at a great distance from Bedfordshire, your Grace may depend upon them for a speedy reinforcement in case of any emergency.'[21]

As we have seen from Luke Francklin's account, Monday 12 September was the day fixed for the swearing in of all those men who had been drawn by lot to serve in the militia. That day was therefore one when further rioting might be expected. On 7 September Lord Royston wrote from Wrest to his father at Wimpole: 'I have received such accounts of the unquiet state of this part of the county, and of combinations in the different parishes to raise a riot on Monday, if not sooner, that I have thought it right to send this morning for a party of the troops from Biggleswade. The meetings on Monday are to swear in the men whose lots are drawn but I am apprehensive, that if mobs once begin on account of the Militia, they will fall to plundering and exacting calamitably (?) as they have done already (as I hear) in some places. I should be glad to have your Lordship's opinion about my conduct on this occasion whether I should stay, or leave the county. There is no personal resentment against me as I have not meddled in the Militia but when a rioting springs up, who knows where it may stop and to what purpose it may be applied. I have writ a letter to Lord Barrington for more troops which your Lordship may need to send away directly if you approve of it. I do not think the troops now at Biggleswade sufficient to protect this county, there being only part of two troops of the Blues. I shall take care to have it known that I do not send for the soldiers to enforce the Militia Bill but to protect everybody, farmers as well as gentlemen in the peace and the enjoyment of their property. The only method to prevent mischief would be to have it known, that the meetings were put off and that nothing further would be done, but I have no authority to give such assurance. I have desired Colonel Sheldon to come over here tomorrow morning that we may consider the affairs together. I should be glad that your Lordship would send on the letter to Lord Barrington, if you approve of it and dispatch the bearer back to me directly. Mr. Birt is alarmed with the apprehensions of danger to himself, although making effort, and no argument I can offer will have prevailed with him to stay.'[22]

Lord Hardwicke replied to this son that evening. His letter was that of a man of considerable political experience. Apart from anything else, he gently reminded his son that he was only Lord Lieutenant of Cambridgeshire and not of the county in which he lived. Hardwicke wrote: 'I am extremely sorry to hear of the continuance, or rather increase of the disturbances and riots in Bedfordshire. Those things are generally aggravated by previous rumours, and yet I fear there is too much ground for apprehension in this case. The Deputy Lieutenants of Hertfordshire were to meet last Monday in a subdivision at Royston to draw the lots. The Hertfordshire mob came and was joined by that of the town, compelled the gentlemen to desist, to deliver them up the lists and to give their word they would act no further into the Act. Parties of them went afterwards to Sir John Chapman's and Mr. Hassell's (two assisting Deputy Lieutenants) broke some of their windows and compelled them to give them drink and money. Though this is within six miles of me, they have not yet marched hither. I have already sent your letter, with one from me, in support of it to Lord Barrington, to be sent from the post house at Royston *immediately* by a flying pacquet which is the most expeditious way of all. I have also, by the same conveyance, writ to the Duke of Newcastle, showed the case to him; and desired his Grace to support your request.

'As I know there is to be a meeting of the King' servants tomorrow night, to consider of these riots and the opposition to the Militia Bill, I have added my opinion that some method should be taken, by private instructions to the Lord Lieutenants, to make hurdles for delay by adjourning the meetings to a long day. That at the beginning of session, the matter may be reconsidered, and perhaps the bill new-modelled into some more practicable shape. In short, if the gentlemen have not the lists, they can do nothing but adjourn; and though nobody is more averse to be giving up laws to popular fury than I am, yet this case is peculiar; because these people, returned and chosen, are to do personal acts by subscribing and swearing; which no body can force them to do, nor do for them, and therefore to raise all this ill-blood, and flame, for the sake of previous acts can end in nothing. As soon as I hear what they resolve, I will let you know.

'You say nothing of your Lord Lieutenant. So is his Grace at Woburn, and if he is, would not he, as Lord Lieutenant expect to have been consulted about sending for more troops? As to your own conduct, I don't well know what to advise. You are now out of the case of acting in this business; and I propound not how you leave the county without adversity nor run any risque. If you leave Wrest, I am of opinion it will be best for yourself to go to London, for that may be supposed to be upon business, on this very affair. Whatever you do, I would by no means leave Lady Grey and the dear little girls, frightened, and Lady Hardwicke and I opine that they will come on hither till the scare is over. All of you will be extremely welcome; and we have full room, but as you are Lord Lieutenant of this county, it may deserve your consideration whether, at this moment you may be at all easier here. I think Mr Birt judged wrong as to himself, and that you gave him right advice.'[23]

Royston took his father's hint and on 8 September wrote to the Duke of Bedford, 'I beg pardon for taking the step I did yesterday without previously acquainting your Grace with it, but I imagined that you were on the point of setting out for Ireland and I doubted the mischief would not admit of delay. I had received such accounts of the unquiet state of this neighbour-hood and of the endeavours carrying on in several parishes around me to raise mobs on Monday, that I thought it right to apply to the commanding officer at Biggleswade for some troops to quarter hereabouts and upon his sending me his answer, that his force was too small to admit of being divided and that the gentlemen would not suffer him to stir, I took the liberty to write a letter to Lord Barrington to desire a greater regular force for this part of the country till things were quieted.

'I returned out of Cambridgeshire on Sunday as our returns from the parishes were not complete. The gentlemen who met as Deputy Lieutenants were unanimously for adjourning our further proceedings till the 13th. of September.

'I am informed that his Majesty's servants are to meet upon this affair of the riots. I sincerely wish they had done it sooner. I have heard of risings from all parts. Mr. Birt is so much alarmed that he is withdrawn from his parish and no arguments of mine could prevail with him to stay.'[24]

That evening Royston wrote once again to the Duke, 'I would have waited upon your Grace and the rest of the gentlemen assembled at Bedford tomorrow but I really think I shall be as usefully employed in sending about the neighbourhood to get the Association signed for preserving the public peace and in talking to the principal farmers and tenants round me . . . to convince them that no force will be used to compel them and that their safety is concerned as well as ours in keeping the country quiet and preventing riots. I beg my lord and doubt not from your Grace's prudence and experience, that quieting methods may be applied till this ferment is a little over and that we have leisure to look about us. I do find the hostility to the Militia Bill very widely spread amongst the middling people. . . . I hope your Grace will make an application for more troops if the number we have appears to be too few.'[25]

Lord Hardwicke wrote a long letter on 8 September to his other son Charles Yorke, who was the Solicitor-General. After passing on the news contained in Royston's last letter Hardwicke gave his shrewd assessment of the troubles. 'But this is become a very serious affair. I understand there is to be a meeting of the King's servants upon it tonight, and possibly you may be advised with. I have writ my opinion to the Duke of Newcastle. Nobody can have a greater detestation than I have, of laws being repealed or set aside by popular dissent and violence. But this is a law, which it is impossible to cram down the people's throats by force. You can never raise a militia by the compulsion of a standing army; in order to do it you may raise a rebellion in the view of raising a militia, to suppress rebellion. All this is absurd. It differs from other cases. Troops may suppress riots and keep up a turnpike. But in this instance, the final acts are to be done by the people themselves personally. They are to subscribe their names and take oaths before the Deputy Lieutenants. No force can make them do that, if they stand out; nor can anybody do it for them. They may indeed be convicted, and be imprisoned or fined for their refusal, but is it possible to imprison or prosecute one thousand or five hundred men in a county at once? Possibly some may propose the issuing of a proclamation to declare the law, and enforce the execution of it; but in my opinion, that would only make things worse and commit the government still more. The proclamation will be waste paper. Force must support it at last; and force is inadequate in the present case.

'Under these circumstances, and as nothing can now be completed for use, my way of thinking is (and so I have told the Duke of Newcastle) that it will be most prudent and advisable to gain time; for which end it may be intimated to the Lord Lieutenants and their Deputies to adjourn their meeting to some long day, as has been done here; and indeed in this county and in many others it may be unavoidable, for so long as all the returns are not brought in, or are forced out of their hands by the populace, the Deputy Lieutenants cannot possibly settle the proportion of men upon the several hundreds and parishes, as the Act directs. If this is done the Parliament will probably meet early in November, and then the subject may be reconsidered and possibly the bill be new modelled into some more practicable shape. If nobody was wiser than I, this should be the provisional measure. The present situation of foreign affairs is a further reason to prevent the growth of these tumults. They will be represented abroad as insurrections, perhaps as a rebellion; at least as disaffection and aversion to assist or serve the government, and great advantage made of it by our enemies.

'I will now tell you what objections that great reasoner, the mob goes upon.

'1.   That they are to serve, on the days of exercise, without pay; and indeed there being no clause for it in the Act, nobody can satisfy them that they are to be allowed any. I always thought it wrong not to insert that provision.

'2.   That when they are drawn by lots and raised, they shall some time or other be sent to serve out of the Kingdom.

'When they are told that there is an express clause in the Act to prohibit it, they reply that they give no credit to that; for that the men raised in Huntingdonshire, and in Devonshire and Somersetshire, in the spring of 1756, were absolutely promised that they should be listed only for three years and not sent abroad, and yet some of them were soon after sent to North America. I fear this is too true; and I always thought it excessively wrong.

'3.   Their third objection goes a little deeper, and must have been put into their heads by somebody. They say the former law laid the burden and charge upon the nobility and gentry and men of property; that this takes it off from them and turns it upon the lower people, who are to live by their labour; and they connect this with their being allowed no pay by the Act, they say it is taking away so much of their bread. I own I have sometimes thought of this, though I never mentioned it; but it has brought to my mind the bargain, which the nobility and gentry made with the Crown soon after the Restoration, when they purchased out their own burdens by the tenures and wardships by laying an excise upon beer and ale to be consumed by the common people, for those liquors, when brewed in private houses, are not subjected to it.

'I have now told you all I know of the fact upon this very disagreeable subject, and the whole of my way of thinking about it. If you like any part of it, you may possibly have some occasion to make use of it.'[26]

Royston's request of 7 September for more troops was forwarded by his father and Tyrwhitt replied promptly on the following day. He informed him of the dispositions already made and added, 'As I apprehend this force will be fully sufficient to answer all the purposes of your Lordship's application, I shall defer sending any more troops into Bedfordshire till I hear that those already there are thought by your Lordship and the other magistrates of the county too few.'[27]

On 8 September Thomas Potter tried to talk to a crowd at Ampthill about the Act. 'Mr. Potter harangued the populace at Ampthill market last Thursday in favour of the bill,' Royston wrote to Hardwicke on the Saturday, 'but without any success, and was hissed out of the town.'[28]

On Friday 9 September the Duke of Bedford held the meeting of the Deputy Lieutenants at the *Swan* in Bedford which Royston had decided not to attend. John Capon (the High Sheriff), the Earl of Upper Ossory, Sir Roger Burgoyne, Sir Humphrey Monoux, Thomas Potter and John Bullock were amongst those who attended. There was an interruption when Monoux was informed that his house at Kempston was in danger from a new mob. A lieutenant of the newly arrived Dragoons with ten men, supported by Monoux, Potter and others, easily put the mob to flight. 'Upon the first sight of the ten soldiers the poor rascals (this near two hundred of them) notwithstanding their great boasting, immediately took to their heels over hedges and ditches, and some into the river, till not a man was to be seen, and the soldiers (having no orders to take them unless they were resisted) returned to Bedford.'[29]

Once reassembled at the *Swan* the Duke and his colleagues decided that as the men drawn by lot in Bedford itself 'obstinately persisted in refusing to be sworn, unless by force', it was pointless to send for them. They also came to the joint conclusion that the county was 'in general so strongly bent in opposition to the Act', that it would be wiser not to hold the further planned meetings until after Parliament had reassembled to reconsider it. All meetings were accordingly adjourned until 28 November.

The question of further publicity was discussed. A short notice addressed 'To the Good People of England' had appeared in the local newspaper the *Northampton Mercury* on 5 September on the instructions of the Duke, explaining the Act shortly, and reassuring the public that no man drawn could be forced to serve abroad. This notice was not wholly satisfactory as Potter, who knew the Act better than anyone, pointed out on 7 September when he wrote from Ridgmont to Edmond Williamson, Rector of nearby Millbrook, enclosing a copy of the notice. 'However I am sorry to find a material omission, for it was ever the intention of Parliament to give the pay of a shilling a day to every militia man for every day he was employed in learning his exercises, and of this you may venture to assure all in your parish.'[30] Potter must have pointed out this omission at the meeting at the *Swan*, for the company resolved to publish another notice. This was to be widely distributed and appeared in the *Northampton Mercury* on 12 September. To give added weight to the notice it was signed by all those present. It read:

'Bedford Sept. 9th. 1757

'We, the Lieutenant, High Sheriff, Deputy Lieutenants and Justices of the Peace for this county whose names are hereunto subscribed, do certify, that according to the best of our judgment, the Act of Parliament for the better ordering of the Militia forces of that part of Great Britain called England, has expressly provided that no private man, serving for himself as a militia man, shall be liable to serve in any of His Majesty's land forces, nor compellable to march out of this Kingdom.

'That although no provision is made by the said Act for the pay of the private man, yet it appears to us, that it is the intent of the legislature to provide such pay as soon as the militia can be properly regulated; for in the clause relative to the pay, arms, accoutrements and clothing, it is enacted that no pay, arms, accoutrements or clothing shall be issued nor any adjutant or serjeant appointed, until four-fifths of the commission officers have taken out their commissions; and as private men cannot be exercised without officers and arms, and the delivery of arms and commencement of pay is comprised in the same clause, it seems to us that the legislature were of opinion at the time of passing the said Act, that no private men should be called out to be exercised until after the Parliament should meet again, when they would have it in their power to make such further provision, as well as alterations and amendments in the said Act, as they should think proper. And as no good subject in this Kingdom can desire a better security for the enjoyment of his rights and liberties than the faith and protection of Parliament, under so good and gracious a King as sits at this time upon the throne of this Kingdom, we esteem ourselves obliged at the same time that we subscribe our opinions with respect to the said Act, to recommend to the serious consideration of every honest man, how much he is obliged in point of his own security, as well as the duty he owes his family, his King and his country, cheerfully to pay obedience to the said Act.

'And that the true meaning of theAct of Parliament may be more fully known and understood, the meetings in the respective sub-divisions for the enrollment of the militia men, are adjourned to the 28th. day of November next.

Bedford	Harry Johnson
John Capon, High Sheriff	J. Franklin
Upper Ossory	J. Harvey
R. Burgoyne	J.M. Dickinson

H. Monoux	Thomas Vaux
J. Crawley	James Smyth
Rob. H. Ongley	John Bullock
John Lee	Thomas Potter.'

On 11 September Potter wrote to Williamson: 'The intention of the in-closed, which I have but this moment received from the press at Northamp-ton, is to quiet the minds of people as to the apprehensions that the militia men were to be sent abroad, and to give notice that though the execution of the Act is not laid aside yet no further steps will be taken till it is fully known and considered. I therefore beg the favour of you to let it be affixed in some public place in your parish where it is most likely to be read this morning.'[31] The other Deputy Lieutenants doubtless distributed copies to their neigh-bours in a similar manner.

As Royston had promised the Duke he would, he at once set about raising supporters for law and order. On 8 September he held a meeting at Wrest Park at which several of his tenants agreed to band together to resist the rioters. He wrote out the following document, of which Edward Horne, senior, made a copy.

'Whereas it has been currently reported that diverse wicked and ill dis-posed persons have threatened to assemble together within this hundred of Flitt, in order to commit the like violences and outrages as have been com-mitted in other parts of this county, we whose names are hereunto sub-scribed, do respectively promise and agree to be ready at all times when we are hereunto required by the magistrates within this hundred, to be aiding and assisting in the suppressing of any and every insurrection or unlawful meeting of the people who shall assemble together to commit any violences or outrages to the disturbance of the public peace within the said hundred.'[32]

The first list was signed by Royston and fifteen others, and fourteen Clop-hill men added their signatures at some stage. The second list was signed by Edward Horne and his son, and by seventeen other Clophill men. Thomas Potter was clearly referring to a similar list when he wrote to Edward William-son on 7 September: 'You have doubtless heard of the disturbances which lately happened near Biggleswade and Potton and of those which happened yesterday below Bedford, and of the treatment which not only the Deputy Lieutenants of the county but several of the clergy and others have received from an ignorant multitude riotously assembled to prevent the laws establish-ed by the King and Parliament from being executed. A meeting of the Lord Lieutenant and all the deputies is appointed at Bedford on Friday morning in order to consider what is fit to be done at this crisis. In the meantime the gentlemen and clergy and substantial inhabitants are forming an association in every hundred and especially in this to prevent the increase of these disturbances. I have inclosed a copy of it signed by myself and intreat the favour of you to communicate it to the farmers and others in your parish and to get it signed by all such as are willing to give their support. I must desire likewise that it may be returned to me tomorrow morning that I may carry it to Bedford on Friday.'[33]

On 10 September Royston wrote to his father to bring him up to date. He assured him that 'agreeable to a hint in your letter of the 7th.' he had acquainted the Duke with his own message calling for more troops. He gave his father an account of the meeting at the *Swan* on the day before, and of the dispersal of the crowd by the Dragoons. After mentioning the signed notice Royston continued, 'This paper I have not yet seen, but do not intend to sign it, as I do not approve the Act. However I have signed an association, which the Duke of Bedford's agents have been carrying about to the different hundreds, for preserving the public tranquility and preventing riots. All my tenants in this neighbourhood have signed it on my recommendation. I have spoken to many of them and shall speak to more as I can bring them to me, on the necessity of putting a stop to these riotous proceedings, and they all seem convinced of it, and have given me the strongest assurances of support. I do not hear that any measures were taken with regard to the Biggleswade riot; I suppose it was too general a scheme to meddle with. I am in hopes that if Monday next passes over here quietly we shall have no more disturbances. . . . The troops will be kept here some time longer and I will write to the commanding officer to have a few in readiness for me if there should be occasion.

'There are some riotous young men in this parish who must be attended to. I told the Duke of Bedford truly in my letter that the bill was disliked much by the middling and lower sort of people in this part of the country. I am amazed that he went so strongly into it as he knows a good deal of the country want of police and subordination.

'He sets out for Ireland tomorrow or Monday. I come now to Cambridgeshire. I am greatly concerned that our adjournment of the general meeting has not prevented riots there, and that they have broke out violently in the neighbourhood of Wimpole. Mobbing is contagious. The Biggleswade tumult communicated itself to Gamlingay and the success of the first riot at Royston has produced the second. I hope your Lordship will keep the troops at Royston for some time longer, and will send and speak to your tenants to be in readiness to assist and defend the mansion house.'[34]

Royston added a most revealing postscript which indicated how much the rioters had succeeded, and how much discretion had proved the better part of valour. 'P.S. The high constable of this hundred residing at Luton, had before the general meeting at Bedford given notice, that there should be no meeting on Monday in our division. I believe that was done by intimation from some of the gentlemen in that neighbourhood. Our lists have been either *privately* given *up* or destroyed, but this I do not *meddle with*.'

On Sunday 11 September both Potter and Hardwicke wrote to their ministerial friends: Potter to Pitt and Hardwicke to Newcastle. The government was certainly put fully into the picture. Potter made it clear that he was ready to take over the duties of the Lord Lieutenant. He wrote to Pitt; 'The Duke of Bedford has left the country, Lord Ossory is gone with him, and Lord Royston, who is the Lieutenant of Cambridgeshire, has declined attending the meeting of the deputies and magistrates of this county. Considering the stake I have in this county, and the very active part I have found it necessary to take for the restoring the public peace and keeping the people within the bounds of their duty, it will not, I believe, be thought presumption, either by you or my neighbours, if I now take upon myself the further conduct of this business, and the execution of any commands which government may think proper to give, in relation either to the past or future transactions.

'Nothing can exceed the terror and apprehensions which the Militia Act has occasioned. . . . . It was in vain that men, the most respected and most beloved in their country, offered to engage their private faith, that no militia-man could or would be sent out of England. The reply constantly was, and it was in the mouths of the women and children, "We cannot believe in this particular, for in this particular even the King's word has been broke; soldiers were raised in Huntingdonshire last year for Abercrombie's regiment, and we hear that the same happened in many other counties; the word and honour of the gentlemen of the country was given in the King's name that they should not go abroad, but were only to be soldiers at home, to fight against the French, and the moment they had taken the oaths they were hurried away from their country, we know not whither."

'This is now the universal language, not only of the meaner people, but of the substantial farmers and yeomen of the country, under whose encouragement, and even in whose pay, the inferior people now rise in rebellion. Yet in this county, though the discontent was universal, the violences, I verily believe, would not have rose to any height but from the unparalleled timidity of those who were the objects of the first attempts. I speak this from what has happened to myself. If I had flown from the country and sent away my family, encouragement would have been given to those who were disposed to commit violences. The contrary conduct has kept everything quiet in these parts; I have rode alone and unarmed into every assembly, and my presence and my persuasions, or at least my threats when they were necessary, have soon dispersed the meeters.

'The Duke of Bedford has acted as became him, and has shown great spirit and activity, joined to great prudence and consideration. On Friday last he met the deputy-lieutenants and magistrates at Bedford: great apprehensions were entertained by the timid, of the violences to be committed that day, and there were found men of rank who confined themselves to their houses, lest, by coming to the meeting, they should be the objects of resentment. Yet the only insurrection of that day I quieted with my own servants, the High Sheriff, and ten of his javelin men, and a party of ten light horsemen from Hawley's dragoons.

'We had another point under our consideration at Bedford. The mob which insulted Sir Roger Burgoyne and Colonel Lee not only committed violence to the public house at Biggleswade, the landlord of which spiritedly refused to deliver up the lists of men left in his custody, but they extorted money from several persons, and in particular from a clergyman, who was no magistrate, nor concerned in the execution of the law, but it seems had from his pulpit recommended obedience to the laws. In this mob it is said there are men of substance, and their names are known, and there is sufficient evidence for their conviction. We thought it not only expedient, but absolutely necessary, that public examples should be made from among the most guilty of these men; but as the same offences may have been committed in other counties, and perhaps have been general, we thought it our duty to delay further proceedings till the King's ministers should come to some resolutions about the measures to be taken.

'It is on this head that I shall be ready to receive and execute the commands of government; and I take the liberty in this manner to offer my services, because it is possible that those commands may fall into hands which are liable to be affected by fear, and may therefore fail in the execution of them.'[35]

On Sunday evening Hardwicke wrote to Newcastle: 'I come now to the affair of the Militia Bill and of the riots. Perhaps the resolution to let things take their natural course and leave the magistrates to proceed as they judge proper, may be the rightest, at least for the present. But then those magistrates must not be blamed for what they shall determine, according to the best of their judgements, upon the circumstances of their respective counties. Mr. Pitt is much mistaken in thinking that the disorders have proceeded *from want of a proper disposition in the Lord Lieutenants and Deputy Lieutenants* to explain the Act, and enforce it. *The whole began in Bedfordshire*, and the infection has been merely communicated from there. The great patron and supporter of the bill in the House of Lords is Lieutenant of that county, and Mr. Potter, the chairman of the committee in the House of Commons, the most active Deputy Lieutenant there; and no activity, explanations, or persuasions, have been wanting. But from Biggleswade the flame spread to Gamlingay, the nearest bordering town in Cambridgeshire, from Gamlingay to the adjoining part of Hertfordshire, and so on.'[36]

The combination of the adjournment of all further meetings, and the presence of troops and their supporters, led to the peaceful passing of the original swearing in day, Monday 12 September. That dangerous day having passed quietly, there was no further rioting. It merely remained for the troops to stay a while to ensure that the King's peace was kept, and for everyone to express their views on the riots.

The Marchioness Grey was clearly interested in her husband's and her father-in-law's views on the Act; her letter to her friend Catherine Talbot on 15 September could have been written by either of the men. 'This Militia Act . . . you object to my calling it absurd. Whether it is absurd to make a law that cannot be executed without force; to force arms into people's hands for the defence of their country, (and by the by what force can make them take the oath of enrolment if they refuse it?) and suppose you can trust to that defence in case of danger. Whether this is absurd I leave anybody to judge, and I must myself add, that it is more than absurd to have tried the experiment and set the whole kingdom in a ferment at such a time as this, and in our present distressed situation. You seem to wonder at your Lord Lieutenant for not doing anything in your county, but I am apt to think it has proved the most prudent action in his life; for in the riotous state your common people were in not long since, this pretence would certainly have revived all former animosities and made them very troublesome. It is too a very bad example, and attended with many bad consequences, I know it here by experience, to attempt the execution of any law and be obliged to give it up to the clamours and riots of the mob. In this case too, most counties have been obliged to call in the assistance of the regular military to defend their houses &c, which this well-constituted militia were to have made no longer necessary in this kingdom. It is certainly much to be wished that some better use could be made of our natural strength. It is very great, but this scheme was impracticable, and most others I fear will prove so, since our people must be reformed before anybody in their senses would choose to put arms into their hands — and *that* reformation is the difficulty. It springs from many causes, and not only from the lives the Great lead in London.

'In this county we are quiet again by the help of troops quartered among us, and by an agreement at a meeting of the Lord Lieutenant and gentlemen held last week under the protection of those troops, to put off all further progress in the affair till November by which time the Parliament may be sitting. Without these temperaments, Monday last week was to have been a great day among us, as it was the day appointed for the men's appearing to be sworn in their respective hundreds, and most of the villages had concerted a regular plan of rising upon that day to destroy the Militia Bill as they said, and go about in triumph to collect money and drink of their neighbours. A great deal of pains was taken to persuade the principal farmers to be quiet, (for in many places they had helped in this discontent) and my Lord was employed all last week in seeing and talking to those in this neighbourhood, and had better success than many others have had: but the troops have proved the most convincing argument, for I am sorry to say, our common people are as cowardly as they are insolent.'[37]

Royston wrote to Hardwicke on 13 September and referred to the Duke's preference for a hard line. 'I hope the neighbourhood of Wimpole continues free from disturbances and that the Blues continue still at Royston as the best security for the county. Everything has been very quiet here since the meeting at Bedford, and I dare say will continue so, as the people understand that the point is given up, and triumph much (as I hear) in having got the better of the Nobility. I send your Lordship a copy of the paper signed at Bedford. I have requested the particulars of what passed, but reports says that the Duke of Bedford was for pushing on with the execution of the Bill but everybody else and Mr. Potter in particular were for adjourning the meetings. I have had very good success in getting the association against riots signed by my principal tenants. They are all very quiet and well disposed.

'Though Blunham is so near the great scene of all this, Biggleswade, I hear but of two persons in that town who joined in it. I should certainly have had the credit of being concerned in the riots had the Bill gone on for Silsoe was to have been the place of rendezvous of some of the neighbouring parishes, and they would have been joined by some silly young men here.'[38]

In his answer of 18 September Hardwicke also had some interesting comments to make about the Duke. 'I think the report likely to be true that the Duke of Bedford was the only person at the meeting for pushing the execution of the Bill. I fear his Grace's driving so fast at first, joined with his unpopularity, contributed to the disorders.'[39]

On the following day Hardwicke wrote to Newcastle once more, making an important point about the prosecution of offenders. 'Prosecution of some ringleaders undoubtedly ought to be, and I am informed that the names of several has been taken down. But if any of them were to be taken up during this ferment, that would undoubtedly be resented.'[40]

Potter managed to give Pitt the impression that his clear head and firm resolution had dealt successfully with protests at Ampthill. Royston pointed out to his father that Potter had been involved in two incidents there, one on 23 August when the lots were drawn, the other on 8 September. In his letter of 23 September Royston wrote with obvious pleasure, 'Mr. Potter's account of the wonderful effects of his eloquence can relate only to the meeting at Ampthill to draw the lots which was held whilst I was in London. There came into the town at that time a body of country fellows with clubs from one of the neighbouring villages, who threatened to break into the inn, where the Deputy Lieutenants were. Mr. Potter went out to them and with good words and giving them money in his own and Lord Ossory's name, sent them away without committing any disturbances. The ill reception he met with from the populace at Ampthill was the day before the meeting at Bedford. I believe he has scarce boasted of the influence of his oratory there, for it is a notorious fact, that he met with very rough answers from the farmers and was hurra'd, not with shouts of applause but of disapprobation out of the market place. Mr. Erskine had attempted to argue the same audience into a better opinion of the Bill just before Mr. Potter made his appearance, and with the same success, as he told me himself. What he did was surely to please the Duke of Bedford, who has provided for both his sons in Ireland. Mr. Potter dined with me on Thursday sennight and then he spoke of the Bill as at an end in this county at least, if not in most others, and some other scheme must be thought of. I am not of the opinion of those who think there has been any management in working up the dislike of the people who have only followed their own natural bias to misrule and mobbing, and the tumult has been so general that no particular influence could extend so universally.'[41]

By 29 September the rioting was so clearly in the past that the Marchioness Grey made a neat joke about it. Her daughter Mary, whose nickname was Mouse, was not yet two, but Lady Grey wrote to Miss Talbot, 'Mouse will be I believe more warlike, and I had thoughts of applying for a commission for her had the Militia scheme taken effect, her great joy at present being noise of all kinds and horses.'[42]

The Government seems to have come to the conclusion that it was best to let matters quieten down before amending the Militia Act, as Potter and others wished. Meanwhile it was clearly better not to inflame the situation by prosecuting any of the rioters. The first amending Act was passed in 1758.[43] The preamble stated, 'Whereas several doubts have arisen and difficulties have occurred in carrying into execution [the Militia Act] and whereas it has been found that some further provisions are necessary, in order to enforce the execution of the said Act. . . .' The new Act reflected the difficulty in obtaining sufficient officers, and the provisions relating to them were amended. One of the more interesting changes was that which permitted the enrolment of volunteers, with a corresponding reduction of the numbers to be selected by lot from the parishes supplying such volunteers.

The preamble to the 1759 Act read, 'Whereas certain counties, ridings and places have made some progress in establishing the Militia . . . but have not yet completed the same, and whereas in certain other counties, ridings and places little progress has been made therein, his Majesty's Lieutenants and Deputy Lieutenants are hereby strictly required speedily and diligently to put the said Acts and this Act in execution.'[44]

On 30 May 1759 Pitt announced in Parliament: 'His Majesty acquaints the House of Commons with his having received repeated intelligence of the actual preparations making in the French ports to invade this Kingdom, and of the imminent danger of such an invasion being attempted, to the end that his Majesty may (if he shall think proper) cause the Militia, or such part thereof as shall be necessary, to be drawn out and embodied, and to march as occasion shall require.'[45]

Six days later on 5 June, the Lord Lieutenants were ordered to get on with the establishment of the Militia. A letter written on 20 July by the Prince of Wales to the King, whom he was to succeed in the following year, indicated how seriously the threat of invasion was regarded. 'Now that every part of the nation is arming for its defence, I cannot bear the thought of continuing in this inactive state. When your Majesty's Kingdoms are threatened, a quiet retreat ill becomes my birth and station.'[46] The King successfully discouraged the military ambitions of his grandson and heir, but the Duke of Bedford was less successful in that respect.

On 8 September the Duke was at last able to report some progress to Pitt. 'In obedience to His Majesty's commands, signified to me in your letter of the 5th. June last, to use my utmost diligence and attention, to carry into execution the several Acts of Parliament made for the better ordering the Militia Force in that part of Great Britain called England, I have the pleasure to acquaint you that I have succeeded so far in this county, as to be able to send you the enclosed list of noblemen and gentlemen who are willing to accept the commissions set against their name, in the list I have the honour to enclose you, and I desire the favour of you to lay it before His Majesty, for his royal approbation. I think it necessary to inform you that Lord Viscount Torrington is by his own particular desire placed as ensign, and as the Battalion is four hundred strong, I think two field officers will be sufficient.'

The enclosure read: 'A list of noblemen and gentlemen who offered themselves as officers in the Militia of the county of Bedford.

The Marquis of Tavistock — Colonel.
Sir George Osborn, Bart — Major.

As Captains

The Right Hon. the Earl of Upper Ossory.
Sir Philip Monoux, Bart.
John Marshe Dickinson, Esq.
Thomas Potter, Esq.
Richard Orlebar, Esq.
George Edwards, Esq.
Ambrose Reddall, Esq.

As Lieutenants
John Franklin, Esq.
Thomas Vaux, Esq.
John Salusbury, Esq.
Thomas Lee, Esq.
Charles Field, Esq.

As Ensigns
The Right Hon. George Viscount Torrington.
George Boheme, Esq.
Joseph Franklin, Esq.
John Hervey, Esq.
Freeman, Gentleman — Adjutant.'[47]

The Duke had mixed feelings about his son and heir, the Marquis of Tavistock, serving in the militia, but there was obviously a limit to how much he could discourage the young man, who wrote that he had a 'rage for everything that has connexion with a military life', and 'I am more militia mad than ever'.[48] Lord Tavistock's madness took different forms: he suggested that the whole regiment of Bedfordshire militia should be innoculated against smallpox at his expense; and when he travelled to Rome at the end of 1761 he even took his scarlet uniform with him — being painted in it by Batoni whilst there.

Although there was rioting elsewhere in the country, notably at Hexham in Northumberland where twenty-one people were killed in March 1761, there was no further trouble in Bedfordshire in connection with the enrolling of the militia, which was embodied for service in March 1760. In June the local regiment marched to camp at Winchester, where it remained until November. In July 1761 the Bedfordshire militia were camped at Sandy Heath near Guildford, returning to Bedford in November once again. At the end of the year, after nineteen months continuous service, the regiment was stood down.[49]

The regiment was not embodied again until early 1778, when Benjamin Franklin succeeded in getting the French to sign a treaty of alliance with the American revolutionaries. The French, who were anxious to avenge their defeat in the Seven Years' War, once more presented a threat of invasion. On this occasion the regiment remained with the colours for five years, being disembodied only in March 1783. Almost exactly ten years later the Bedfordshire militia men were called to the colours again in view of the new war with France. Fortunately there was never any repetition of the troubles of 1757.

All references are to documents in the Bedfordshire County Record Office unless otherwise stated.

1. J. W. Fortescue, *History of the Army,* London: Macmillan, 1899, Vol.2, p.290.
2. Raymond Postgate, *"That Devil Wilkes",* London: Constable, 1930, pp.81, 57; when Wilkes was first arrested in 1763 in connection with his *North Briton* No. 45, in which he criticised the Bedford/Bute treaty, the use of a general warrant for his arrest was said to be legal by the Attorney-General of the day, Charles Yorke, who had consulted his father, Lord Hardwicke.
3. *Correspondence of William Pitt, Earl of Chatham,* London: John Murray, 1838, Vol.1, p.173.
4. 30 Geo. II c.25, Section 51.
5. FN 1253, p.116 ff.
6. *B.L.* Add. MSS 35,351, f.383.
7. Lord John Russell, *Correspondence of John, Fourth Duke of Bedford,* London: Longmans, 1843, Vol.2, p.383.
8. L 30/9a/7 p.240.
9. *B.L.* Add. MSS. 35,351, f.393.
10. *P.R.O.* WO 1/974, p.39.
11. *Ibid.* p.35.
12. *P.R.O.* WO5/44, p.468.
13. Tony Hayter, *The Army and the Crowd in Mid-Georgian England,* London: Macmillan, 1978, p.12.
14. Lord John Russell, *Correspondence of John, Fourth Duke of Bedford,* London: Longmans, 1843, Vol.2, p.267.
15. L 30/9a/7 p.256.
16. *B.L.* Add MSS 35,351, f.400.
17. *P.R.O.* SP 44/189 p.432.
18. *Herts. C.R.O.,* D/EP f.267.
19. *P.R.O.* WO1/973 p.105.
20. FN 1253 p.152.
21. *P.R.O.* WO 4/54 p.411.
22. *B.L.* Add. MSS. 35,351,f. 402. Philip Birt was the vicar of Flitton, and usually a very conscientious magistrate.
23. *Ibid.* f.405.
24. Record Office of Northern Ireland, T 2915/2/54.
25. *Ibid.* p.53.
26. *B.L.* Add. MSS. 35,353, f.222.
27. *P.R.O.* WO4/54 p.413.
28. *B.L.* Add. MSS. 35,351, f.410.
29. FN 1253, p.155.
30. M 10/2/81.
31. M 10/2/82.
32. L 29/24 *and* 25.
33. M 10/2/81.
34. *B.L.* Add. MSS 35,351, f.410.
35. *Correspondence of William Pitt, Earl of Chatham,* London: John Murray, 1838, Vol.1, p.257.
36. *B.L.* Add. MSS 32,874, f.4.
37. L 30/9a/7, p.262.

38. *B.L.* Add. MSS 35,351. f.415.
39. *Ibid.* f.417.
40. *B.L.* Add. MSS 32, 874. f.146.
41. *B.L.* Add. MSS 35,351. f.419.
42. L 30/9a/7 p.268.
43. 31 Geo. II c.26.
44. 30 Geo. II c.25.
45. *History, Debates and Proceedings of both Houses of Parliament,* London: Debrett, 1792, Vol.3 p.433.
46. Bonamy Dobrée, *The Letters of King George III,* London: Cassell, 1968, p.14.
47. Sir John M. Burgoyne, *Regimental Records of the Bedfordshire Militia from 1759 to 1884,* London: W. H. Allen, 1884, p.2.
48. Georgiana Blakiston, *Woburn and the Russells,* London: Constable, 1980, p.129.
49. Burgoyne *op.cit.* p.7 *et seq.*

II
THE VERSATILE PHILIP HUNT

There can be few Bedfordshire characters who led fuller lives or who were more versatile than Philip Hunt, yet until recently he has been largely overlooked by local historians. Joyce Godber made no mention of him in her classic *History of Bedfordshire 1066-1888*, published in 1969, although she did refer to him several times in *The Harpur Trust 1552-1973*, which appeared four years later. The present writer produced a short sketch of Hunt for the *Bedfordshire Magazine* in Summer 1975, and described in detail his work as a visiting justice in the county jail in *A Study of Bedford Prison 1660-1877*, which was published in 1977.[1]

Hunt had, however, figured importantly in William St. Clair's excellent book, *Lord Elgin and the Marbles*, published by Oxford University Press in 1967. The author's preface began, 'By far my greatest debt of gratitude is to Mrs. A. C. Longland of Abingdon who unreservedly made me a present of a collection of papers which belonged to her great-grand-uncle Dr. Philip Hunt. These papers first aroused my interest in Lord Elgin's embassy.' He also acknowledged his indebtedness, as does the present writer, to Arthur Hamilton Smith, who had used Hunt's letters to Elgin in his long article on 'Lord Elgin and his Collection' in the 1816 *Journal of Hellenic Studies*.[2] The writer asked Mr. St. Clair whether he would allow the County Record Office to take copies of his papers, and he very kindly agreed to do so.[3] Now is perhaps an appropriate time for Hunt's story to be told more fully than before, and for convenience in four sections. The first will cover his time with Lord Elgin; the second, his connection with John Russell, 6th. Duke of Bedford; the third, his prison work; and the fourth will discuss his contribution as an expert witness. There is one serious omission: Hunt as a churchman does not merit a separate section, as there is relatively little evidence relating to that important aspect of his life.

1. As Vol. 56 of the Publications of the *B.H.R.S.*, and in hardback by Phillimore.
2. Vol. 36, pp. 163-372, hereafter cited as Smith.
3. The County Record Office reference is Microfiche 30; the documents are hereafter cited as Hunt Papers.

HUNT AND LORD ELGIN

Philip Hunt was born on New Year's Day 1772 in Herefordshire and went to school in Newcastle-on-Tyne, where his father had business interests. He was admitted to Trinity College, Cambridge, at the age of sixteen, graduating in 1793, and becoming Rector of St. Peter Martin, Bedford, in 1799. He remained Rector of St. Peter's, as it is now known, for thirty-six years, but was absent from his parish for the first few years on the grandest of grand tours, which took him to Constantinople, Athens, Venice, Paris and Dublin. Dublin was not on most grand tours, but Hunt travelled there after seeing the more exotic cities, and before settling down to his work in Bedford.

In 1799 Thomas Bruce, 7th. Earl of Elgin, was appointed ambassador to Turkey. On the recommendation of his friend, Thomas Brand, the Rector of Maulden, Hunt was given the post of chaplain by Elgin. The young cleric was delighted, writing to his father at Ludlow from Ampthill on 2 April, 'I have consulted Lord Ossory and my other friends here, who all concur in describing it as a most brilliant opportunity of improving my mind and laying the foundation of a splendid fortune . . . it will be certainly attended with great present advantages and most probably lead to an independent fortune.'[1] Even though Hunt may not have taken a vow of poverty, his reaction was a very earthly one, as his father probably pointed out to him. The parental strictures seem to have had some effect, for on 17 July the son replied in confessional terms from Cheapside in the City of London. 'Your obscure hints have already made me scrutinize the recesses of my mind, and I trust that the investigation has been attended with some good. I found many defects in my conduct, and I hope I also found good principles, and resolutions to practise any virtues, or eradicate any improprieties that you may point out, and which have escaped the attention of one who fears he has been too flattered by partial friends.'[2]

The young man soon learned that Elgin was not going to make him rich in the near future, and that he would have to cut his coat according to the Cloth. He reported to his father sadly on 28 August from Portsmouth, 'I had fondly indulged the idea that from the instant my connection with Lord Elgin commenced, I should cease to be under the necessity of applying to you for money, but I have found a serious reverse. Nor do I imagine I shall receive any part of my salary till after the conclusion of our embassy. Mr. Hammersley, banker in Pall Mall, who is a neighbour of Mr. Gould [Hunt's nephew] at Northaw, has supplied me with a letter of credit, which will enable me to draw for any sum I may want during our absence from England, and I have found Mr. Gould very kind in letting me have cash for my expenses in London, which have much exceeded all ideas I had formed on the subject.' He added, 'Our ship is a frigate of thirty guns, and in consequence of her having only one deck we shall have much worse accommodations than I could possibly have imagined; our cots swing so close to each other, that they must necessarily touch on every motion of the ship.'[3]

In a later letter Hunt elaborated on the accommodation.[4] 'The morning disclosed a scene which should afford a good subject for the pen of Swift or the pencil of Hogarth. In our little cabin twelve feet long, six broad and 6½ high, were five beds, five gentlemen, 13 large trunks, 8 small do., 6 basons &c., 6 hats, 5 dressing gowns, 5 greatcoats and boat cloaks, 3 servants getting ready our shaving apparatus and a cabin boy brushing shoes; 5 foul cloathes bags, 4 portmanteaux, 2 pewter bottles, 2 lanterns, 2 umbrellas, a travelling library, brooms, supernumerary blankets, quilts, brushes, carpets &c. in most glorious confusion, and an eighteen-pounder with its tremendous apparatus of carriage tackles, iron crow, balls and grape shot.' Fortunately for the travellers, the food was much better than the accommodation. 'The captain's table on board our frigate is most excellently supplied; and by the quantity of live-stock of every description with which he has furnished himself, we have regularly two courses at dinner, nor have we yet had more than a single dish of salt beef.'

In the same letter Hunt informed his father that a delay in setting sail from Portsmouth had enabled him to go sightseeing, taking in a view of the prison ships in which he was to acquire a near professional interest in due course. 'We sailed from Portsmouth on Thursday September 3rd. after having been detained long enough by contrary winds to allow us to view the dockyard, the prison ships and other subjects connected with the British navy, which astonished me by their grandeur, as well as by the regularity with which they were conducted.'

Lady Elgin, who was pregnant, had a very bad time crossing the Bay of Biscay, and stayed below on the first Sunday out, but she reported to her parents, 'Hunt read the service on deck. . . . Hunt preached a sermon; Elgin said it was a good one.'[5] The captain of the frigate, H.M.S. *Phaeton*, put into Lisbon for a few days to allow Lady Elgin to recover. She wrote from there on 15 September, 'We have had an earthquake the night before last. It was the most violent one they have had for these three years past. It did not wake me, but it shook down little Hunt's bed, and plump on the floor he landed with an amazing crash.' On the following day Hunt, who had come down to earth with a bump in more senses than one, wrote to his father, 'I began to ruminate on the novelty of my situation and I must own I felt somewhat of a depression of spirits, when I considered that I was entering into a new sphere of life in which talents might be required that I do not possess.'[6] From Gibraltar he wrote a letter in which he asked his father to remember him to the Goulds, 'and my prime favourite Frances, and the rest of the dear little folks'. His niece, Frances, or Fanny Gould was to look after Philip Hunt when he was approaching his end. The letter continued with more ominous financial news. 'Tell Mr. Gould that I fear I shall have occasion to make use of Mr. Hammersley's letter of credit, as our ambassador has never troubled himself with enquiring into the pecuniary concerns of any of the party, and has left us hitherto to bear all our own expenses and cautiously avoids any allusion to so paltry a consideration.'[7]

After Gibraltar the ship put into Palermo in Sicily, where Lord Nelson was making himself at home with the British Ambassador, Sir William Hamilton, and, more particularly, with his wife Emma. Lady Elgin expressed her disapproval of the *ménage à trois*, but Hunt kept his views to himself. On the other hand, he was prepared to comment once more on Elgin, writing from Sicily on 19 October, 'Though Lord Elgin's conduct towards me does not quite come up to the ideas I had formed, yet I hope to reconcile myself sufficiently to whatever occurs, and not suffer any disgust to prevent me from enjoying the many enviable circumstances that my situation embraces.'[8]

The journey continued through the Eastern Mediterranean, and on 1 November the party landed on the mainland of Asia Minor. Five days later they arrived at Constantinople, where they received a warm welcome. Hunt explained to his father on 9 December, 'In consequence of the great services we have lately rendered the Turks, the name of Englishman procures the most profound respect and the most flattering attentions from every person connected with the Ottoman Government.'[9] The pressure of work on all members of the embassy staff was great from the outset. As various secretaries were sent off on official business, Hunt was persuaded to take on work of a clerical nature not usually undertaken by a cleric. 'In the absence of Lord Elgin's Secretary of Embassy, and of his other secretaries employed on different missions, a great deal of public business, connected with the embassy, devolved on me, so as entirely to occupy my time,' he complained later.[10] Lady Elgin wrote to her parents as early as 18 November to express her concern about the extent of her husband's work. 'It is really enough to turn one's head to see him and his business at present, such packets from India have arrived, him, Morier and Hunt are the whole day writing.'[11]

Hunt became extremely unhappy about the demands made on him by Elgin and wanted to return home. He later wrote, 'To me his Excellency, from the early part of our intercourse, behaved so differently from what my hopes, perhaps too sanguine, had anticipated, that I soon felt my situation in the British Palace at Pera very irksome, and requested leave to quit the embassy and return home, but by persuasion of my friends and the desire of being useful to my country in the important affairs that had arisen from the war in Egypt, the interest of which was daily increasing, I was induced to comply with his Excellency's urgent request of remaining in his suite till the close of the embassy.'[12]

One of the tasks with which Hunt was concerned was the sorting and dispatch of the effects of a young Scots scholar, John Tweddell, who had died on his travels. Years later both Hunt and Elgin were to have cause to regret their encounter with his estate, for Tweddell's brother was to mount a vitriolic attack on them. Another scholar played an important part during Hunt's early days with Elgin. He was Joseph Dacre Carlyle, Professor of Arabic at Cambridge. His entry in the *Dictionary of National Biography* suggests that he was Elgin's chaplain, but that appointment was, of course, Hunt's. Carlyle was attached to the mission so that he might search for ancient manuscripts in various ecclesiastical establishments. 'The plan originated with Mr. Pitt and the Bishop of Lincoln,' Hunt wrote later, 'who thought that an embassy sent at a time when Great Britain was on the most friendly terms with the Porte, would afford great facilities for ascertaining how far these hopes of literary discovery were well founded.'[13] He continued, 'During our residence at Constantinople, Mr. Carlyle and myself visited all the monasteries of the Greek monks, or caloyers, on the Princes' island in the sea of Marmora. Their names are Principo, Chalke, Prote, Antigone, Oxya, Platya. The manuscripts in their libraries did not contain a single classical fragment; but there were many copies on paper and vellum of different parts of the New Testament, written apparently about the 11th., 12th. and 13th. centuries; the most beautiful of these we bought from the monks, who used printed books in the service of the church, and attach little value to their ancient manuscripts. These are now deposited in the Archbishop of Canterbury's library at Lambeth.' Hunt added that other manuscripts, which they had found in the library of the Patriarch of Jerusalem in Constantinople, were also at Lambeth.

Having scoured the local libraries, Carlyle and Hunt went further afield. Carlyle was originally going alone but accordingly to Hunt, 'Mr Carlyle's health had suffered so much during his residence in Turkey, that he would not venture alone upon a journey to Macedonia, in order to examine the libraries of the Greek convents on the peninsula of Athos; he requested, therefore, that Lord Elgin would allow me to accompany him. We preferred going by sea, as we might thus have an opportunity of visiting the plain of Troy, and the islands of Tenedos and Lemnos. We procured a firman or official permission from the Porte for travelling in Asia Minor and Greece, and a recommendatory letter from the Greek Patriarch to the Council of Deputies, who govern the religious community at Mount Athos.'

The two men left Constantinople for a short sea journey on 3 March 1801. They were doubtless properly equipped for their expedition, for the Hunt Papers contain some of their hints for later travellers. The advice included the following fashion notes for anyone venturing into the interior: 'The Tartarian or Polish dress will be found the most convenient. In this case a defence for the eyes will be wanted; and the best is made with a piece of pasteboard cut into the shape of a crescent, covered with green silk and bound round the front of the cap by means of a silk ribband.'

In his journal of the trip with Carlyle, apart from anything else, Hunt revealed his botanical interests. On 6 March 'another valley opened upon us. The season of spring was now commencing, and every patch of grass was covered with anemones of the most vivid hues, scarlet, white and blue: these were intermixed with the crocus, asphodel, hyacinth, and purple orchis; on the hills the variety of shrubs was very great. We saw the arbutus, andrachne and unedo, the sweet bay, the ilex, the wild olive; many kinds of broom, heather, the spina christi, wild vine and clematis.' Some of his finds may now be reproduced in this country, for on 22 July Lady Elgin wrote home, 'Hunt has given me a number of different seeds that he has collected. I have got a tin-box made and shall, by the first opportunity, send them'[14]

Hunt's account of the journey shows both how exhausting and how rewarding the experience could be. On 6 March they reached the village of Jouragec towards sunset. 'As the accommodation for sleeping consisted only of a dirty mat and an uneven mud floor, we were not induced to pass a long night at Jouragec. We therefore set off at three o'clock in the morning by moonlight, and riding through extensive woods we again came to the shores of the Hellespont.' The travellers had breakfast at 11 a.m. at the house of a Greek priest, but were soon on their way. 'At a quarter past twelve we resumed our journey. . . . We reached the town of the Dardanelles about seven o'clock in the evening.' They had their reward on the following evening. 'The sun was nearly setting when we reached the foot of Cape Yenicher, the ancient promontory of Sigeum. The ascent was steep, but when we had mounted towards the top we had the gratification of a fine view of the plain of Troy, the winding course of the river through it, the island Tenedos beneath us; Samothrace and Imbros, and Lemnos on our right, with a faint view of the Pike of Mount Athos on the opposite continent in the fading distance of the horizon.' A little further on the two clerical travellers had a shocking experience at Boyuk Bournarbashi. 'We found this town very gay and noisy on account of the celebration of a Turkish wedding, and before we retired to rest, a band of musicians, who had been brought to the wedding feast from the Dardanelles, came to our lodgings with a set of dancers. . . . The dance was altogether so indecent, that we soon dismissed them.'

On 21 March Hunt and his companion arrived on the island of Tenedos, and there the Rector of St. Peter's turned his enquiring mind on to a most important topic for a gentleman. 'The principal and almost sole produce of Tenedos is wine. . . . The red kind is strong, and as dark and rough as port. A small quantity of muscadel is also made, which is much esteemed; the red sells at eight paras, or fourpence the oke of 2¾ lb.; the white muscadel at thirty.'[15] Next came Lemnos, and finally, the Athos peninsula. Hunt described their arrival graphically. 'After our tedious abode at Lemnos, and the violence of the storms which we had experienced, we were gratified in no common degree with the view of the convent of Batopaidi, embosomed in the midst of gardens, woods and meadows. We had reached a small creek at the foot of it, but the surf was so high that we scrambled with difficulty over the rocks, and as soon as we landed we pursued a road which led us through groves of lemons, oranges and olives, to the monastery. On reaching the gate we found that approach more like that of a fortress than the peaceful abode of monks. The lofty walls were flanked with towers, and many cannon appeared at the embrasures. The outer gate was doubly plated with iron; a long dark winding passage led from it, in which were two guns on carriages and three more gates secured by strong bolts and bars.'[16]

The formidable defences were designed to keep out pirates rather than travellers such as Hunt and Carlyle, and the two men duly spent five days at this first monastery examining the manuscripts kept there. From Batopaidi they moved on to all the others on Mount Athos, being offered assistance in their search at each place. Hunt referred to the well known rule that no female creature was allowed on the peninsula and pointed out the breaches of that rule. 'The superstitious or artful caloyers repeat gravely to every stranger who visits them, that no female animal could live three days on Mount Athos, although they see doves and other birds building their nests in the thickets, swallows hatching their young under the sheds, and vermin multiplying in their dirty cells and on their persons.'[17] Incidentally, once Hunt left Mount Athos he was delighted by females — despite his disapproval of the dancing at the marriage feast. Soon after leaving Athos he came to a place where 'we saw a number of women in the fields weeding the corn and singing; the sight of female dresses, and the voices of these sun-burnt daughters of labour, were most pleasing after having lived so long among the monks of Athos.'[18]

Hunt and Carlyle searched all the libraries on the peninsula, but found very little of interest in them. On the other hand, the total experience was clearly most interesting and not all hardship. Hunt recounted that they dined at Iverson monastery with the ex-patriarch Gregorio, who had been in exile there for two years. 'We found his table furnished in a style quite ex-conventual, with lamb, sausages, ham and French wines. His dispensing power seems to remain although he is dethroned; and seven or eight of the salad-fed monks who dined with us appeared to be much pleased with their change of diet.'[19]

Carlyle also kept a diary of the trip, and he reported an incident when Hunt was a victim of crime — not for the last time. 'A young man of Constantinople, who spoke Italian and whom we found at the convent, had been in some degree useful to us as interpreter. He had attended us in the library and called upon us afterwards. He admired an omnium gatherum belonging to Mr. Hunt, and at the moment Mr. Hunt's back was turned he fairly stole it. The business however was too barefaced and we obliged him to return it.'[20]

From Mount Athos the two men travelled to Salonica and then to Athens, a journey which led to two narrow escapes from pirates. In Athens Hunt went sightseeing with Lady Elgin's parents, who were on their way home after visiting their daughter in Constantinople. On 22 May 1801 Hunt wrote to Elgin, 'They were so kind as to include Mr. Carlyle and myself in all their parties; and I am convinced that no travellers have spent a short period on this classic soil with more external advantages. Mr. Nisbet's connexion with your Lordship opened to us the gates of the Acropolis and every recess of the superb buildings it contains; and guided by so able a Cicerone as Lusieri, as well as by the local knowledge which your Lordship's architects and modellers now possess, the Athens of Pericles seemed to rise before me in all its pristine beauty.'[21] As this letter indicates, Elgin had for some time had a team of artists sketching and making plaster casts of various antiquities. Giovanni Battista Lusieri was the principal artist, one J.M.W. Turner having declined the offer of that post. Historically the most important passage in Hunt's long letter to his employer was that which contained the following advice: 'Positive firmans must, however, be obtained from the Porte, to enable the architects and modellers to proceed in their most interesting labours. Unfortunately, the Temple of Minerva, called the Parthenon, and those of Neptune Erechtheus, of Minerva Polias, and Pendrosos, as well as the famous Propylea, are all within the walls of the Acropolis, now a Turkish fortress, garrisoned by mercenary and insolent janissaries, so that every obstacle which national jealousy and Mohametan bigotry, seconded by French intrigue, could produce, have been too successfully used to interrupt their labours. Till those firmans are obtained, the bas-reliefs on the frieze, and the groupes on the metopes, can neither be modelled nor drawn.'

On 4 June the British embassy in Constantinople celebrated the King's birthday, and on the following day Lady Elgin wrote to her mother. 'Who should arrive yesterday in the middle of our Grand Fete but Mr. Hunt! Never was traveller more heartily welcomed. He is in the highest of spirits.'[22] On 1 July Hunt drafted a memorandum in which he elaborated on his views about the need for a specific legal authority from the Turkish government. He wrote: 'Mr. Hunt recommends that a firman should be procured from the Porte, addressed to the Voivode and Cadi of Athens, as well as the Disdar, or Governor of the Citadel; stating that the artists are in the service of the British Ambassador Extraordinary, and that they are to have not only permission, but protection in the following objects:

1) To enter freely within the walls of the Citadel, and to draw and model with plaster the ancient temples there.
2) To erect scaffolding, and to dig where they may wish to discover the ancient foundations.
3) Liberty to take away any sculptures or inscriptions which do not interfere with the works or walls of the Citadel.'[23]

Elgin's interpreter, Pisani, in due course tried to get the Turks to fall in with Hunt's suggestions, but not before undergoing a minor crisis. Pisani claimed that overwork had affected his health, and — like Hunt before him — expressed a wish to resign from Elgin's service. There were clearly problems other than those caused by overwork, for Lady Elgin wrote home on 7 July that her husband had given Pisani 'a most amazing rattle'.[24] She continued, 'Upon this, Hunt became mediator and explained exactly what E. expected of him, saying that E. insisted upon his translating literally whatever he gave him, without Pisani's taking upon himself to alter his orders, by way of pleasing the Turks. After a long confab, Pisani thanked Hunt for his friendship and promised all that man could promise.' Hunt's peacemaking soon paid dividends, for on 9 July Lady Elgin reported, 'I am happy to tell you that Pisani has succeeded *à merveille* in his firman from the Porte. Hunt is in raptures, for the firman is perfection.' And so it was, for it was clearly based on his draft of 1 July.

The original Turkish version of the firman has not been traced, despite Mr. St. Clair's efforts to track it down, but an Italian translation of the document, in Pisani's handwriting, is with the Hunt Papers.[25] The document concluded with the command, 'It is our desire that on the arrival of this letter you use your diligence to act conformably to the instances of the said Ambassador as long as the said five artists dwelling in that place shall be employed in going in and out of the citadel of Athens which is the place of observation; or in fixing scaffolding around the ancient Temple of the Idols, or in modelling with chalk or gypsum the said ornaments and visible figures; or in measuring the fragments and vestiges of other ruined buildings; or in excavating when they find it necessary the foundations in search of inscriptions among the rubbish; that they be not molested by the said Disdar nor by any other persons; nor even by you to whom this letter is addressed; and that no one meddle with their scaffolding or implements nor hinder them from taking away any pieces of stone with inscriptions and figures.'[26]

On 10 July Elgin wrote to Lusieri, his principal artist, in enthusiastic terms, 'Mr. Hunt will tell you how much we have thought about the means of coming to your help, and will show you better than I can describe, the proofs of the efficacious measures that we have taken — I refer to him for all the details. . . . The journey that Mr. Hunt is undertaking offers a field for your talent and taste that has never before been offered to any artist. The places he is going to visit, the support he will have everywhere, his zeal, his intelligence, and his knowledge being all equally favourable, promise a most happy end to this excursion.'[27] The journey to which Elgin referred was of a diplomatic nature, and not merely in connection with antiquities. Hunt explained his new task in a letter of 8 July to William Richard Hamilton, the embassy secretary, then on a mission in Egypt. 'I have no news, either foreign or domestic, to add to this farrago, except what you must open all your eyes and ears to attend to – it is that my Reverend Self am about to set out from hence as a kind of diplomatician to the Morea, Albania, and such other parts of European Turkey as we have certain information are menaced by Bonaparte. . . . The object of my mission is to create an impression in favour of our views, and of our power; to state to the different agents of government in Morea, Albania &c. what we have done, and what we are capable of doing, to protect Turkey against foreign invasion, to repress the rebellions, and encourage the faithful and loyal subjects of the Porte.' It sounds almost as though the Rector of St. Peter's had been converted to Islam! His bubbling letter continued, 'On such classic ground, investigations into the remains of antiquity, and an attempt to procure such as are interesting and portable, will naturally come in as a secondary object; and as I shall carry a firman to enable our artists to prosecute without interruption their researches in the Acropolis of Athens, I will take care to see it put properly into execution.'[28]

Elgin also gave Hunt some commercial duties. On 14 July the ambassador wrote; 'Besides these more immediate objects, it is of the highest importance that you should direct your attention while on this excursion to the present state of commerce, to the natural productions, and to the degree of security which may reasonably be expected by the English in mercantile transactions, in the countries through which you may pass. The quality of timber, and the facility and expense of cutting and transporting it to a place of embarkation, are objects which occur as deserving a particular enquiry.'[29]

On his new journey to Athens Hunt stopped at Gallipoli and there admired an inscribed column. He wanted to copy the wording, but discretion proved the better part of valour. 'It contains a Greek inscription which I could not with prudence stop to copy in a crowd where the plague was suspected,' he wrote to his employer.[30] There were further hazards to be overcome on the journey. On 31 July he reported to Elgin from Athens that one of his fellow-passengers on board ship, 'happening luckily to go on deck about midnight, saw a latine-sailed vessel rowing towards us, in hopes, I make no doubt, of finding us asleep or at least unprepared. In a moment all was bustle, we cleared for action, distributed muskets, and concealed ourselves till the vessel came within hail. The speaking trumpet was given to me, as English is supposed to have more effect on the nerves of a Maniote than lingua franca.' A broadside from Hunt, albeit in the dreaded English language, was not sufficient to make the pirates sheer away, so the captain had to resort to cannon fire, which did the trick.

In the same letter Hunt reported the success of his meeting with the Governor of Athens, and of the firman. 'When the Vaivode had read the letters, and perceived the determined tone with which we spoke, he became submissive to the extremest degree, and assured us he was highly mortified to find that the Disdar had presumed to treat any Englishman with disrespect, or demand any money. . . . The conference ended with repeated assurances that henceforth the gates of the Citadel are open to *all* Englishmen, from sunrise to sunset, and to draw or measure any of the old buildings they please, and that your Lordship's artists are to consider themselves at full liberty to model, dig or carry away whatever does not interfere with the works.'

This conference proved to be a turning point, thanks in part to the zeal with which Hunt flung himself into the work of removal of ancient remains. His letter continued, 'Today the ship carpenter and five of the crew mounted the walls of the Temple of Minerva, and by the aid of windlasses, cordage, and twenty Greeks, they succeeded in detaching and lowering down, without the slightest accident, one of the statues or groupes in the metopes representing a combat between a youth (probably Theseus) and a centaur.' 'I do not recollect to have ever felt my heart throb with greater violence, than when I saw this treasure detached from the entablature of the Parthenon, and depending on the strength of Ragusan cordage,' Hunt wrote at a later date.[31] As A. H. Smith has commented, 'The next few days must have been days of feverish activity.'[32] By 28 August Lady Elgin was able to write home, 'Elgin has had letters from Hunt, and all has been managed better than we could have expected at the Temple of Minerva.'[33]

On 21 August Hunt sent a detailed account of his Athenian activities to the Earl of Upper Ossory. 'My second visit to this celebrated city has been attended with circumstances equally honourable to the English nation and to Lord Elgin's embassy. Hitherto access to the temples in the Acropolis has always been difficult and attained only by bribes to the Governor, demanded in a manner equally arbitrary and insolent, and proportioned according to the supposed rank or eagerness of the individual. Your Lordship will be glad to know that in consequence of the remonstrances I made here in the Ambassador's name, he had been able to establish the right of every English visitor to enter the citadel freely at all hours of the day, and not only to examine the ruins, but to sketch them. . . . In addition to this his Excellency's artists are allowed not only to model and draw the public buildings, but to make excavations among the ruins in search of statues &c, and to clear those parts of the temples that were defaced by heaps of rubbish or modern walls. It grieved me to the heart to see the destruction wrought daily by the janissaries of the fortress. They break off the finest bas reliefs and sculptures in search of the morsels of lead that unite them to the building, after which they are broken with wanton barbarity.'[34] And so the Parthenon was demolished to protect it from demolition. To Elgin Hunt wrote, 'These admirable specimens of Grecian sculpture which have been repeatedly refused to the gold and influence of France in the zenith of her power, I have now embarked with other precious fragments of antiquity, on board the ship that brought me here.'[35] Hunt gave rather more details about the shipping arrangements when he gave evidence to the Parliamentary Select Committee considering the Elgin Marbles in 1816. He related how he had shown the firman to the Governor, who had responded favourably, 'in consequence of which I asked him permission to detach from the Parthenon the most perfect and, as it appeared to me, the most beautiful metope. I obtained that permission and acted upon it immediately: I had one carefully packed and put on board a Ragusan ship which was under my orders, from which it was transported to a frigate and sent to England.'[36]

On 2 August Hunt left Athens on his mission 'as a kind of diplomatician'. On his travels he was much assisted by the very cooperative Governor of Athens. 'He sent me continual presents of provisions and fruit, and gave me government post-horses for all my excursions,' Hunt wrote to Elgin on 3 September.[37] On 9 September he sailed for Egypt on board a Ragusan brig, taking with him two metopes from the Parthenon and other items collected in Athens. After a very long and tedious journey during which he suffered a great deal from fever and ague, Hunt arrived at Alexandria. There the small collection was handed over to the Royal Engineers for onward transmission to England. Hunt returned to Constantinople but was not permitted to rest for long. On 28 March 1802 he left for Greece once again, this time in company with the Elgins, who were anxious to see some of the places about which he had given such enthusiastic accounts. After several months in Greece they returned to Turkey once more, journeying overland from Smyrna. On 8 September, after her safe arrival at the embassy, Lady Elgin wrote to her mother about that last stage. 'Pray tell my Father *I* manoeuvred the troops consisting of fifty people for five days. . . . Hunt will tell you I am the best general ever was seen.'[38]

Hunt left Constantinople for the last time on 15 November 1802. Elgin sent him to Greece to report on the movement of Bonaparte's emissary, Colonel Sebastiani, although the war with France had been ended by then by the Peace of Amiens. This mission to Greece also enabled him to check on progress in Athens, and to try and help with the salvage operations on the wreck of the *Mentor*, which had foundered whilst carrying many of Elgin's prizes. Three days before his departure from Constantinople Hunt wrote a letter to his employer about any possible reward for this final mission. 'In answer to your Lordship's request of my setting out immediately for Athens, in order to execute certain instructions with which you are to furnish me, I have only to say, that as Greece is a country which I have repeatedly visited, and in which I can now hope for little personal gratification, I am induced to undertake the voyage solely from the hope with which your Lordship flatters me, of my thus being able to render some essential public service.'[39] Hunt assured Elgin on 19 December that he was remaining inconspicuous in his task of shadowing the French colonel. 'The loss of the *Mentor* and your Lordship's antiquarian researches will furnish me with reasons sufficiently plausible for my journey.'[40]

On Christmas Eve Hunt reported to his employer from Athens that the British ship *Braakel* had run aground nearby on the previous day, and had been in danger of breaking up. 'I immediately repaired to the Vaivode, and on observing the phlegmatic slowness with which he was going to execute my request of sending down a hundred men, I spoke in the name of his Majesty, and insisted on the gates of his residence being instantly closed by the Arnaout Guards, and the requisite number pressed for service out of the gaping multitude of Greeks and Albanians who were in the courtyard.'[41] The ship was soon lightened and was safely brought into port. Hunt was able to add some good news about the master, who was clearly grateful to the Rector-cum-salvor. 'Captain Clarke seems disposed to take on board everything that is ready for him, and the stay he must now necessarily make to recover his guns &c. will give Lusieri time to get not only the Ionic columns from the Temple of Venus at Daphne, but every other marble in the magazine. Your Lordship has been fortunate in thus getting so roomy a ship, and a captain so disposed to serve you.'

Early in the New Year the Elgins left Turkey for the last time and joined Hunt in Athens. On 3 February they sailed together for Malta on the journey home. Hunt decided to travel independently through Italy and France, and he and the Elgins were still on the Continent when the war restarted on 23 May 1803, and when Bonaparte ordered the detention of 'all the English enrolled in the Militia from the age of 18 to 60, holding a commission from his Britannic Majesty'. As ill-luck would have it, the decree was interpreted in such a broad manner that both Elgin and Hunt were detained under its provisions.

It was not until August that Lady Elgin was able to report to her mother what had befallen Hunt. 'Poor Hunt, at last we have heard from him. He went with Mr. Pink to Venice, crossed Mont Cenis, and being assured he might safely go through France, they proceeded, but were stopped at Montmelian, where Hunt had a severe fit of illness. He petitioned for leave to go to Lyons, Paris or Geneva for medical advice, but was refused. Elgin has written to Paris to ask for permission for him to return to England; if that should not be granted, to allow him to join us.'[42] Hunt's continued absence from his parish was considered by the Bishop of Lincoln, who on 27 January 1804 gave him a further two years permission to be absent 'on account of your being a prisoner in France, and consequent inability to return to the duties of your cure.'[43]

On 14 February Lady Elgin wrote that Hunt was at the house which Elgin had taken at Pau, near the Pyrenees. Her letter included the odd comment,

'The roses are in full bud and Hunt eats violets with his bread and butter every morning.'[44] Further letters reveal the fact that whilst Elgin and Hunt had a relatively comfortable period of detention in France, both were for a short while confined on political grounds, Hunt being kept at Bitche in the Castle of Tears, as it was known to its inmates. Whilst at Pau, the men were hardly troubled, and were only required to report to the authorities occasionally. Even if Elgin did not like Hunt much — and he certainly did not like paying him — he seems to have felt obliged to assist him in his plight. Lady Elgin on the other hand clearly had a soft spot for the clergyman: her references to him were all couched in friendly terms. For example, on 26 February 1805 she wrote from Pau, 'I am glad to see that the Bishop of Norwich is made Archbishop of Canterbury. . . . Perhaps some time or another, he will do something for Hunt; how happy that would make me if one could get a nice thing for him as a surprise.'[45] In that month Hunt wrote a long letter to Lady Elgin's mother, with whom he had gone sightseeing in Athens, giving a detailed account of 'what was done by Lord Elgin's artists at Athens and other parts of Greece, after you left us'.[46] Another version of that letter was used by Elgin as the basis for his own *Memorandum of the Earl of Elgin's Pursuits in Greece,* which was first published in 1810.

In March the party left Pau and travelled to Paris, where the Elgins' youngest son, William, died. Elgin persuaded Bonaparte to allow Lady Elgin to return home, so that the child might be buried in the native soil he had never seen. At any rate, that was the basis of the request, and it succeeded. Hunt was permitted to escort the sad mother and her child out of France.[47] And so Hunt regained his liberty after more than two years in captivity and returned to England in October 1805 after an absence of six years. Elgin had to wait until the following June before he was freed. It seems likely that Hunt and his former employer then had an unpleasant discussion about any financial rewards due to Hunt, and possibly also about any counterclaim that Elgin might have in respect of the period in France. In 1816 Hunt wrote, 'I had (by 1813) been for some years, as I still am, estranged from all habits of intimacy or intercourse or acquaintance with that nobleman, owing to circumstances in which the public can now feel no interest.'[48] Elgin had indicated their distaste for each other in 1815, by writing, 'The fact, however, is that from circumstances of a very peculiar and painful kind, I have had no connection or intercourse with Dr. Hunt since a period long anterior to these declarations.'[49]

The reason that both men had referred to each other in print, was that both had been attacked in the preceding year in a book entitled *The Remains of John Tweddell,* written by his brother, Robert Tweddell.[50] John Tweddell was the young scholar whose belongings Hunt had helped to send back home after his early death. Robert Tweddell accused both Elgin and Hunt of making unauthorised use of his brother's papers, and he made the most of the fact that in response to his enquiries the two men had given somewhat inconsistent answers. This was scarcely surprising in view of the lapse of time.

Whilst Elgin, Hunt and Tweddell were exchanging allegations and counter-allegations in print on the issue of the Tweddell relics, the question of the manuscripts obtained by Hunt and Carlyle was raised. We have already seen that some had been deposited at the Lambeth library of the Archbishop of Canterbury, and there they had remained, even though mainly lent for inspection purposes. Some of the manuscripts are still in the Archbishop's library, and Mr. St. Clair has rightly pointed out that Hunt must take some of the blame for the fact they were not returned speedily.[51]

When Elgin and Hunt gave evidence in 1816 to the Select Committee which was investigating the question of purchasing the marbles for the nation, they probably studiously avoided one another. They probably did not even discuss the problems created for them, with differing degrees of seriousness, by the antiquities, the Tweddell brothers and the monastic manuscripts. Hunt clearly could not stand Elgin. One must add, in fairness to Elgin, that without the opportunities his mission gave to Hunt, the latter's life would have been much duller. The six years which the Rector of St. Peter had spent away from his cure were clearly extremely rewarding, despite the absence of any significant financial reward, and despite the two years' detention in France. Hunt had not only had the experience of extensive travelling, but also of diplomacy and other subjects not usually coming within the province of an English cleric. Apart from anything else, the six years he had in the service of the Earl of Elgin fitted Philip Hunt admirably for his next task, as secretary and chaplain to John, Duke of Bedford.

1.   Hunt Papers.
2.   Hunt Papers.
3.   Hunt Papers.
4.   Hunt Papers, letter to father, 16 September 1799; cp. the cabin scene in the classic Marx Brothers film, *A Night at the Opera.*
5.   Nisbet Hamilton Grant, *The Letters of Mary Nisbet, Countess of Elgin,* London: John Murray, 1926, p. 9, hereafter cited as Grant.
6.   Hunt Papers.
7.   Hunt Papers.
8.   Hunt Papers.
9.   Hunt Papers.
10. Earl of Elgin, *Letter to the Editor of Edinburgh Review,* Edinburgh: Manners and Miller, London: John Murray, 1815, p. 58.
11. Grant, p. 46.
12. Philip Hunt, *A Narrative of what is known respecting the literary remains of the late John Tweddell,* London 1816, p. 12.
13. Robert Walpole, *Memoirs Relating to European and Asiatic Turkey,* London: Longman, Hurst, Rees, Orme and Brown, 1917, p. 84 ff; hereafter cited as Walpole.

14. Grant, p. 101.
15. Walpole, pp. 124, 129.
16. Walpole, p. 198.
17. Walpole, p. 204.
18. Walpole, p. 225.
19. Walpole, p. 208.
20. *B. L.* Add. Mss. 27, 604 f. 33.
21. Smith, p. 186.
22. Grant, p. 90.
23. Smith, p. 190.
24. Grant, p. 96.
25. St. Clair, pp. 89, 90.
26. Hunt Papers.
27. Smith, p. 191.
28. Smith, p. 193.
29. Hunt Papers.
30. Smith, p. 194 ff.
31. Grant, p. 330.
32. Smith, p. 196.
33. Grant, p. 105.
34. Hunt Papers.
35. Grant, p. 123.
36. *Parliamentary Papers,* 1816, Vol. 3.
37. Smith, p. 200.
38. Grant, p. 217.
39. Hunt Papers.
40. Hunt Papers.
41. Hunt Papers.
42. Grant, p. 259.
43. *Beds. C.R.O.* P 100/0/14.
44. Grant, p. 309.
45. Grant. p. 348.
46. Grant, Chapter 21.
47. St. Clair, p. 132.
48. Philip Hunt, *A Narrative of what is known respecting the literary remains of the late John Tweddell,* p. 12.
49. Earl of Elgin, *Letter to the Editor of the Edinburgh Review &c.,* p. 18.
50. It was published by Joseph Mawman, who had taken over the business of the well-known publisher from Southill, Charles Dilly.
51. St. Clair, p. 249.

HUNT AND THE DUKE OF BEDFORD

John Russell, who became 6th. Duke of Bedford, was a Whig Member of Parliament for Tavistock from 1788 until he succeeded his brother Francis in 1802, when he was translated from the House of Commons to the Lords. When the Administration of All the Talents was formed by Fox and Grenville in 1806 Whig politicians, after many years in opposition, at last had a chance of holding office. Samuel Whitbread was one of the leading Whigs who was disappointed not to be chosen for any post at all, but the Duke of Bedford was offered, and accepted the post of Lord Lieutenant or Viceroy of Ireland, one which his grandfather, the 4th. Duke, had filled with distinction many years earlier. We do not know how the Duke came to select Hunt as his secretary and chaplain to accompany him to Dublin, but Hunt must have been feted in the county in the few weeks between his return from captivity in France in October 1805 and the appointment of the Duke on 12 January 1806. In any event, the Duke did appoint Hunt, who had two qualifications in addition to those already mentioned. First, he was a Whig supporter, and secondly, he was a very broadminded man in religious matters, who could not stand bigotry. As the Duke was keen to overcome some of the anti-Catholic laws, Hunt's broad outlook was probably helpful. Whilst in Dublin with the Duke for a period of a little over a year Hunt was appointed Secretary for Ulster and Munster. The Ulster post doubtless entailed rather less work than that falling on the present-day Secretary of State for Northern Ireland.

The issue which led to the early fall of the government in 1807 was one which had been raised by the Duke, and taken up in London by his colleague Lord Howick, Whitbread's brother-in-law, soon to be 2nd. Earl Grey. Grey is remembered now principally for the Reform Act of 1832, of which he and the Duke's son, Lord John Russell, were the principal architects. At the end of 1806 there was considerable unrest in Ireland, and even some rioting. The Duke made a number of proposals for measures to appease the Irish. One of his suggestions was that Roman Catholics should be able to hold the military rank of colonel, not only in Ireland, but also in the rest of the British Isles. George III was hostile to the idea of Catholic emancipation and told the ministers that he would not tolerate the proposed reform. He went on to insist that his ministers should assure him that they would take no further steps to improve the lot of the Catholics. This intolerance on the part of the King, who was supported to some extent by public opinion, led to the resignation of the government. One of the junior ministers, the playwright Richard Brinsley Sheridan, commented, 'I have known many men knock their heads against a wall, but have never heard of any man who collected the bricks and built the very wall with an intention to knock his own brains against it.'[1]

After the fall of the government the Duke returned to Woburn. He was clearly well pleased with Hunt's services in Ireland, for he invited him to join him and his family on a long tour of Scotland later in the year. On 3 August 1807 the young Lord John Russell wrote in his diary, somewhat formally, 'I left Woburn Abbey in company with the Duke and Duchess of Bedford and the Rev. Dr. Hunt.'[2] On 18 August, his fifteenth birthday, Lord John wrote, 'I went with Dr. Hunt to Walter Scott's house.'

Hunt did not stay long in the employ of the Duke, and soon settled down to a quarter of a century or so as the working Rector of St. Peter's. However, he devoted himself to many other interests as well as his church. Amongst other things he became a magistrate and a Harpur Trustee. Miss Godber has demonstrated in her history of the Trust the important contribution made to education in the town by Hunt who, according to her, 'took his trusteeship seriously'.[3] It is clear that Hunt had very broad views on education, and so it comes as no surprise to learn that when a meeting was called in the town in 1829 to consider the establishment of a public library, he was elected chairman.

In 1822 the Duke published a beautifully illustrated book cataloguing his own collection of marbles, *Outline Engravings and Descriptions of the Woburn Abbey Marbles.* The illustrations were by Henry Corbould, and the text was by that authority on Greek antiquities, Philip Hunt, although his name is nowhere mentioned in the book. It is clear from the Hunt Papers that he was the author and also from a letter the Duke wrote to his son, Lord William Russell in 1825. 'Thanks for executing commission at Paris about the Breguet. It is intended as a present for Dr. Hunt as a mark of my gratitude for the trouble, anxiety and care he took in drawing up the descriptions of my marbles, and moreover to compensate for the loss of his own which became the booty of the London brigands, alias pickpockets.'[4] The Breguet was, of course, a watch made by the famous French watchmaker, Abraham-Louis Breguet. It was doubtless on the strength of his authorship of the Woburn marbles book that Hunt applied, successfully, to become a Fellow of the Society of Antiquaries in 1828. Sir Robert Inglis, the Chairman of quarter session, was one of his three sponsors. Despite this, Hunt was later to make a bitter attack on Inglis in a letter to the Duke.

We shall see later that in 1827 Hunt gave evidence to the House of Commons Select Committee on Criminal Commitments and Convictions which had been appointed on the suggestion of Lord John Russell, and which was chaired by him. In the following year Hunt expressed some concern to the Duke about his other son, Lord William, who was not paying sufficient attention to the affairs of the Bedford Corporation. In chiding his son the Duke wrote, 'You will not suspect [Dr. Hunt] of being unfriendly to you or to me.' Lord William certainly did not think Hunt unfriendly, for on 29 March 1828 he wrote in his diary. 'Having slept and breakfasted at Dr. Hunt's — a worthy good clergyman — rode to call on Samuel Whitbread, who is very ill'.[5] St. Peter's Rectory was clearly a place suitable for a visit by a Duke's son. The same could scarcely have been said before 1817, when Hunt had supervised the rebuilding. On 26 January 1813 the Bishop of Lincoln had given the rector a licence to be absent for two years 'on account of the insufficiency of the house of residence for the residence of a clergyman'.[6]

Hunt was unlucky with his other ecclesiastical homes also, for three weeks earlier he had been granted permission to live away from his post as Vicar of Ravensden because of the 'unfitness of the house of residence'; and a year later he received a similar licence in respect of his living as Vicar of Willington. St. Peter's Rectory was in due course pulled down to make way for the Junior School of Bedford School, but not before Hunt's successor, the Rev. G. Burnaby, and his wife had had a son there, who became the celebrated Colonel Fred Burnaby.[7] Hunt's experience with the rebuilding of the rectory, and his involvement with building works at the county jail, encouraged him to make alterations to the church itself, together with its surroundings. The local historian J.H. Matthiason wrote in 1831, whilst Hunt was still rector, 'The whole range of buildings has been so restored and beautified as to present not only a very pleasing but an elegant appearance.'[8] Two years later Matthiason had an opportunity of assessing Hunt's range of prison buildings when he was imprisoned for debt.

In 1833 Hunt at last obtained the 'nice thing' from the Archbishop of Canterbury for which Lady Elgin had hoped back in 1805: he was made a prebendary Canon of Canterbury, although he remained in Bedford until 1835. In the Public Record Office are two letters from Hunt, from The Precincts, Canterbury, which confirmed that he was a Whig still, and that he still abhorred bigotry. The first, dated 21 March 1836, was to the Duke, who visited him in that year.[9]

'My dear Lord Duke

It was not till this afternoon that I was able to obtain a sight of Dr. Hampden's admirable inaugural lecture. Our bigotted high Tory chapter takes no other newspaper than the atrocious Standard: though some individuals among them add the John Bull to strengthen them in their exclusive illiberality, and the Standard after unmeasured abuse of Dr. Hampden as a Heretic and Deist refuses to print his defence, pleading first that it must be a contamination of his heterodoxual opinions — and in a second paper that the lecture is a complete refutation of his former opinions and that they will not give currency to any productions of a man so unstable in his religious creed. I hope Ld. M. will continue firm, and we shall soon see these Oxford bigots sink into deserved contempt. Sir Robt. Inglis should be their Chancellor, High Steward and Representative in Parliament, and Sir Harcourt Lees should be their Secretary! I really believe there is some baneful contagion arising from long residence in Oxford, that unfits men for their duties to general Society. I would never select a Bishop from those who have never left College, but kept themselves aloof from all sympathies with better men than college walls contain. I have obtained a promise of assistance in the duties of Easter Sunday — I preached yesterday to a large congregation as poor Mr. Moore was quite unequal to the effort.

'I have the honour to remain very truly your Grace's obliged servant.

'P.S. My newly-made little garden is looking beautiful.'

Hunt's references to the Oxford bigots is interesting. We have seen that the Duke and he had been involved in a Whig attempt to lessen the discrimination against the Catholics thirty years earlier. When the Whigs finally regained office under Grey in 1830, their reforms alarmed both the opposition and the Church of England. Where would these wretched reformers draw the line? Even the Church of England might not be spared. The Oxford Movement, with John Henry (later Cardinal) Newman as a leading light, grew partly out of the anxiety about possible attacks by the Whigs on the established church.

The second letter, dated 9 October 1836, was to Lord John Russell, the recently appointed Home Secretary.[10]

'Dear Lord John,

In consequence of the Duke of Bedford having passed some time under my roof at this place, and the long patronage with which he has honoured me, there are many individuals who persist in thinking that I must have influence with your Lordship with respect to the appointment to offices in your department and though I resist many applications made by such persons yet I cannot always refuse them without appearing to have deserted a cause which I have much at heart, allow me therefore to suggest to your Lordship that much care is requisite in the choice of two magistrates or justices of the peace for this city: as it is imagined that the Lushington Tory Party want to infuse some bigotted and intolerant partizans into the number of those now in the Commission. The present justices (at least as well as I can ascertain their sentiments) seem to think that if you were to add the names of William Masters, Esquire, an alderman, and William Mount, Esquire, probably an alderman also, to the actual number of justices all would be well and the liberal cause secured. Mr. Masters is an eminent nurseryman well known to the Duke of Bedford, not only professionally but as a man of great reading and much scientific knowledge, his Grace having seen much of him here and having invited him to visit Woburn Abbey. I also know him well as a strenuous and able supporter of liberal principles and the advancement of science, literature and the fine arts, but in his religious opinions I hear that he is what is here called Latitudinarian and Heterodox.

'Of Mr. Mount I do not know much except that his character is respectable, his manners quiet, and that he is esteemed as a friend by the Liberals: he is by profession a land agent, steward and surveyor and it is stated to me that he would make a good city justice. I remain my dear Lord John your Lordship's obliged servant.'

Hunt's relationship with Elgin had been terminated as soon as both men were free to disengage from one another, but his friendship with the Duke of Bedford and his sons clearly lasted for thirty years.

1. Philip Ziegler, *Addington,* London: Collins, 1965, p. 268.
2. Spencer Walpole, *Life of Lord John Russell,* London: Longmans Green, 1889, Vol. 1, p. 31. The doctorate was one of Laws, and had been conferred on Hunt by Dublin University.
3. J. Godber, *The Harpur Trust, 1973.*
4. Georgiana Blakiston, *Lord William Russell and his Wife 1815-1846,* London: John Murray, 1972, p. 97.
5. Blakiston, p. 159.
6. *Beds. C.R.O.* ABA 2/3.
7. A. Cross, *Links with Past Bedford: S. Peter de Merton,* Bedford, 1905, p. 47.
8. J. H. Matthiason, *Bedford and its Environs,* 1831, p. 32.
9. *P.R.O.* 30/22 2A p. 314.
10. *P.R.O.* 30/22 2C p. 235.

HUNT AND BEDFORD PRISON

Hunt was appointed a county magistrate in 1811 and from 1815 until his retirement in 1835 he was intimately concerned with the running of the county jail and house of correction. His rectory was close to the prison buildings, but that proximity alone is not enough to explain the extent of his involvement. Sidney and Beatrice Webb pointed out how much valuable work was done throughout the country by clerical justices, but Hunt clearly surpassed most of his colleagues.[1] It is likely that Hunt's fellow justices soon realised that they had a colleague who was not only able, but also ready and willing to cope with the many thankless tasks falling onto those of their number who were appointed as visiting justices for the penal institutions of the county. It was as a visiting justice that Hunt interested himself in prison matters for the twenty years during which Thomas Warner was jailer. The writer has dealt in detail with Hunt's relationship with Warner in Chapters 7 and 8 of his history of the prison. In a review of the book in *The American Historical Review,*[2] Frank F.Foster suggested that those two chapters 'present a strong case for including Reverend Hunt among the important early-nineteenth-century prison reformers'.

At the time of Warner's appointment to the post of jailer in 1814 Hunt demonstrated his dislike of bigotry and his appreciation of some of the qualities required of a jailer. The post was vacant because of the dismissal of John Moore Howard, who had held it since 1783, and one of the first applicants wishing to replace him was Captain J. Mitchell, the adjutant of the Second Regiment of the Bedfordshire Local Militia. Mitchell wrote to Samuel Whitbread, whom he knew to be an influential magistrate as well as the commanding officer of the First Regiment, pointing out that he was 'of the Church of England', whereas a rival applicant called White was not only a dissenter, but 'as big a Jacobin as any one'.[3] He added that Hunt was a friend of his, so Whitbread, who was shocked by this letter, passed it on to the cleric. Hunt replied, 'I beg leave to thank you for your kind and candid communication of a letter written by Captain Mitchell, in which he has introduced my name in a manner quite unauthorised by me: and I have no hesitation in adding that his scurrilous abuse of his competitor has given me a most unfavourable opinion of himself. Captain Mitchell was the first candidate who called upon me for my recommendation to the Sheriff as a fit person to fill the office of jailer. He mentioned having obtained the decided support of Lord St. John to whom he had been long and intimately known; and that the Chairman of the sessions had assured him that he thought him particularly well qualified for the situation. He also alluded to being opposed by a candidate who was not a member of the Church of England, and spoke of his own services in the Army and local military corps of this county. To all this statement I only said that as the situation of jailer was of great importance to the police and morals of the county, and required great integrity, steadiness, and unremitting attention, I should decline promising my support to any candidate until I had a conference on the subject with my brother-magistrates; and that when we had examined the pretensions of all the candidates, I should give my vote most conscientiously in favour of him who appeared best qualified for the able and faithful discharge of the office.'

Hunt concluded: 'I beg leave to add that if he had spoken to me of his competitor in the language used in the letter you inclosed to me, I should have required no other argument to make me suppress even the wish I expressed that a person burthened with so large a family as his, might prove the most meritorious candidate on this occasion. For I could not bear to see the unfortunate inmates of a prison under the control of a person of such illiberal and un-Christian sentiments as Captain Mitchell's letter contains'. The post went to Thomas Warner, who had been the sergeant-major in Whitbread's regiment.[4]

Although one would have expected a Whig clergyman of the early nineteenth century to have been an opponent of slavery, it is nevertheless interesting to see that the man who was to be so important to Bedfordshire prisoners was a keen opponent. Hunt had witnessed Elgin's successful efforts in Turkey in 1802 to secure the release of the Porte's Maltese slaves.[5] In 1814 he made his own small contribution. On 20 June 1814 he wrote to Whitbread, 'You have probably been informed that the Mayor of this town has called a meeting of the inhabitants, on Wednesday the 22nd. of this month, to congratulate the Prince Regent on the signature of the Treaty of Peace; and as I am anxious that the address should not be unworthy of the town which has the honour of being represented in Parliament by so strenuous an asserter of the rights of humanity as yourself, I take the liberty of inclosing you a copy of the address I propose to bring forward, as it contains an allusion to the abolition of the infamous traffic in slaves, which ought to be urged at the approaching Congress with all the influence Great Britain has acquired by her conduct during the war, and her moderation in arranging the terms of peace, as far as her own individual interests were concerned.'[6] His address included a suggestion that Great Britain should call for 'the immediate and total abolition of the odious, cruel and infamous traffic in slaves'.

The end of the Napoleonic Wars was followed by an increase in crime everywhere, and the county jail, which had been built in 1801 for about forty prisoners, was at times required to house eighty or even a hundred. The county justices became disturbed about the overcrowding and dispatched Warner to see how their colleagues in Warwickshire coped. On his return the jailer presented a detailed report, which he doubtless discussed with Hunt.[7] On 3 September 1818 quarter sessions appointed a committee to examine the problems of the jail and of the house of correction, which was contained in the same building. The Duke's eldest son, the Marquis of Tavistock, attended the first meeting on 14 September. Hunt was not only a member of the committee, but also drafted its report which was dated 21 October, for which quarter sessions duly thanked him.[8]

In the report Hunt drew attention to the overcrowding and pointed out that it 'completely prevents any attempt towards that separation, which is essentially necessary to a system of reformation and good prison discipline; and the practice is so contrary to cleanliness and health, that typhus fever has frequently spread to considerable extent within this prison. It has indeed occurred, in more than one instance that youths committed to the present house of correction in the course of last summer, and arriving there in good health, have returned home with fever of a contagious kind, contracted in prison. Fatal results have followed, and the inhabitants of the villages, to which the unfortunate offenders returned, have designated the disease by the name of jail fever.'

Understandably, Hunt was concerned with the moral as well as physical well-being of the young prisoners. He was concerned about youngsters being corrupted by the experience of imprisonment – a matter still concerning many people today. His report continued: 'In this mixed and crowded state of the criminal prisoners it is obvious that not only the moral and religious feelings of the individuals confined must be irretrievably injured, but that the mischief extends to the labouring classes throughout the country at large, amongst whom the demoralized culprits return; because the present house of correction (which is not even effectually separated from conversation with the felons' yard) is the place to which boys convicted of misdemeanours in service, runaway apprentices, and young men unable to find sureties in cases of bastardy, or trifling assaults, are lodged for months, and instead of its proving to them a penitentiary, or a place productive of reflection and reformation, and adapted for learning or forming good principles and good resolutions, it is a sink of corruption, in which the young and comparatively innocent are brought to associate with hardened and notorious offenders, whose evil communications and depraved habits familiarize them with a knowledge of crime; and when these young persons go back to their villages, they become corrupters of others, and are probably linked in intimacy with those dangerous friends who were their companions by day, and sharers of the same cell or perhaps of the same bed at night.'

Hunt went on to suggest the adoption of four principles:

'First, a proper separation and classification of offenders.

'Secondly, means of employment and reformation to those who are not hardened in crime.

'Thirdly, such confinement, seclusion and hard labour as may prove a sufficient terror and a real punishment to notorious and hardened offenders.

'Fourthly, the preservation of such good principles of honesty and religion as youthful delinquents may still possess, when for the first time they enter a house of correction.'

Two alternative solutions were suggested for the resolution of the existing difficulties. The first possibility, it was suggested, was to provide for the separation of various classes of prisoners in the existing building. In addition to that there would have to 'be built in some eligible and central part of the county a penitentiary, or place of confinement and reformation, totally unconnected with the present prison, and appropriated exclusively to persons unable to find sureties for the peace, or in cases of bastardy, or assaults or affrays, or non-payment of a small penalty, or for misdemeanours in husbandry-service, or in apprenticeship, or first conviction under the game laws, or similar petty transgressions.'

The second option, Hunt advised his colleagues, 'in the event of that which has been now detailed, being thought likely to fix too heavy an expense on the county, is to add such a pentitentiary as has been described to the present jail, there being sufficient ground for such purpose on the north side thereof and which is the property of the county; and that it should contain, as far as may be practicable, all the necessary arrangements for a detached house of correction, having a separate entrance on the west side, for the admission of its peculiar prisoners, and also a door communicating with the present jail'.

The report, in two later sections, refers to Hunt himself in a manner which indicated the extent of his powers as sole visitor. 'Indeed escapes from this prison have been so frequently attempted, and have so often succeeded, that the visiting magistrate has provisionally ordered a night watchman, well armed, to perambulate the walks of the prison, until the next adjourned meeting of the justices in session; and he strongly recommends such an appointment being permanent for the winter months at least.' 'The visiting magistrate has also, with the approbation of the committee, ordered walls, instead of palisades, to be built along the passage leading from the turnkey's lodge to the jailer's house ...... so as to prevent the prisoners from seeing every person who enters the jail.'

The report concluded with a passage which is still extremely relevant. Hunt stated that Warner, the jailer, 'is convinced that prisoners generally leave his jail and bridewell more wicked than when they were first placed under his care.' He continued: 'Indeed, it is well known by those who have noticed the conduct of young offenders after their discharge from bridewell, and on their return to their respective parishes, that they are so much more depraved as to excite regret at having sent them there; and magistrates, in consequence, frequently recommend complainants to forbear from urging the conviction and commitment of young persons, unless the misdemeanour be of a very aggravated kind, considering that the impunity thus granted to such youths is less dangerous than sending them to such a school of vice and corruption.'

The excellence of Hunt's report led to his name coming to the notice of the government as that of a justice whose views were worth obtaining. The principal Whig spokesman on penal affairs in the House of Commons was The Hon. Henry Grey Bennet, who in 1816 had married Lord William Russell's daughter, Gertrude. Shortly after the appearance of Hunt's report to quarter sessions Bennet wrote a long letter on penal matters to Lord Sidmouth, the Home Secretary, who as Henry Addington had been Prime Minister. At the end of 1818 Bennet published a copy of his letter, which contained considerable criticism of Home Secretaries, but praise for Hunt.[9] Bennet quoted from Hunt's report, which, he wrote, was 'drawn up with great care and precision by that zealous and intelligent magistrate, the Rev. Dr. Hunt'. The two men had probably met at Woburn through the Russells, or through a mutual association with Whitbread.

Quarter sessions opted for the second of the proposals: the building of a new house of correction on the site adjoining the existing jail which had been built in 1801 — a site which is incorporated within the wall of the present prison. Unfortunately, the architect chosen, James Elmes, who was the editor of the *Annals of the Fine Arts* and who rather fancied himself as an expert on prison architecture, designed the most appalling building. This created rather more problems than it solved.[10] The new house of correction was opened on 12 April 1820, but it failed to solve the problem of over-crowding. In their return to the Home Secretary in the following year the justices reported, 'Built originally to contain thirty-seven, with a separate cell and bed for each male; but with the number of prisoners having greatly increased, the beds have been enlarged, and by putting two persons in one bed, the prison was made to contain fifty-two.'[11]

At times when one reads the quarter sessions records one gets the distinct feeling that Hunt's colleagues took advantage of his anxiety to be helpful, and of the fact that he lived close to the jail. For example, when Elmes reported the completion of his disastrous building, quarter sessions ordered, 'that a new garden fence be placed at the new house of correction, and that the same be done under the direction of Dr. Hunt'.[12] Two years later a prisoner escaped from the new building during the night. By eight a.m. the keeper was fetching Hunt to look at the empty cell.[13]

On 23 January 1823 Hunt wrote an official letter to the Under-Secretary, Henry Hobhouse, about the 'discipline mill with treadwheels', which had been installed in the new house of correction in 1821. 'I beg leave to add that the justices of this county are so thoroughly convinced of the superiority of this species of labour for prison discipline, that they have ordered a similar mill with tread wheels to be erected and worked at the old house of correction for this county, in addition to the mill now there, which is worked by crank machinery'.[14] The old house of correction was a part of the main jail building. On the same day Hunt wrote another letter to the Home Office about a visit he had paid to the new Brixton house of correction (also still in use!), and he made some critical comments about the treadmill there. The Home Secretary in due course published both of Hunt's letters in a report entitled *Comments respecting the Use of Treadwheels.* Hunt was very annoyed about the publication of his second letter — the Brixton one. When on 23 March 1824 he wrote to Sir Robert Peel, the new Home Secretary, he headed the letter *Private* and wrote, 'I hope I shall be pardoned for requesting that this letter may be considered Private, so as not to be printed, as on a former occasion, when I accompanied my official letter respecting the tread wheel labour with a private letter, pointing out what I conceived to be a defect in certain wheels in some other prisons, that letter which I intended to be *private*, was printed with my official one as a visiting justice.'[15]

Peel was largely responsible for the two Prison Acts of 1823 and 1824, which laid down detailed rules for the separation of different classes of prisoners. Hunt contributed to the discussions which preceded both Acts, and he clearly had sufficient technical expertise to be able to make some worthwhile suggestions.[16] The requirements of the two Acts were so stringent that the Borough of Bedford, which had its own jail and only a few prisoners, could no longer comply with the law. As a result, in 1824 the Borough entered into a contract with the county, which provided for the county to detain Borough prisoners in future, for eight shillings a week per head.[17] Hunt represented the county during the negotiations.

Hunt's humanity may be gauged to some extent by the various punishments which he ordered for attempted escapes or other prison offences, and by his readiness to reduce penalties or to recommend a remission. One illustration must suffice. On 23 June 1826 Warner reported to Hunt that James Walker had smashed up his cell.[18] He was placed in a 'straight waistcoat', but succeeded in tearing that into shreds. Walker, who was no newcomer to the jail, admitted his offence and was sentenced to one week in the refractory cell, to be followed by three weeks solitary confinement with a mattress on the floor only. Three days later Hunt's entry in the visiting justices' book read, 'The Rev. Dr. Hunt visited the prisoner and on James Walker's expressing his sorrow for his irregular and violent conduct, and his resolution to behave well in future, he was allowed the indulgence of sleeping in one of the common cells during the remainder of his week's confinement to the refractory cell.' Four days after this 'the jailer reported that the conduct of Walker during his confinement in the refractory cell has been tranquil — and as no further violence is apprehended from him, the jailer is allowed to furnish his cell with a bedstead'. Hunt must have been disappointed by the way in which Walker may be said to have repaid him. Soon after his release from jail he was caught with James Yarrow stealing a horse. Partly on the strength of Yarrow's evidence for the prosecution, Walker was convicted at the Lent Assizes in 1827 and sentenced to death. Yarrow was 'so abused and insulted by his comrades' for having turned King's evidence, that Hunt had him sent to a different ward, and wrote to the Secretary-at-War 'to send a file of soldiers to remove James Yarrow as a deserter'. Walker was executed at the jail on 31 March 1827. Cases such as this doubtless made Hunt wonder from time to time whether his efforts were sufficiently appreciated by the prisoners.

In 1827 Hunt got in touch with the Home Secretary once more. This time the subject-matter was a question of criminal statistics, and the letter must have been one of the first to deal with that topic. On 19 February Hunt wrote to Peel, 'I beg most respectfully but most earnestly to direct your attention to the subject of your circular letter, addressed to the clerks of the peace, for returns of the convictions that have taken place under the Game Laws during the last seven years, as I fear those returns must necessarily be so deficient as to give a most erroneous impression as to the enormous increase of offences of that nature, it being the practice of magistrates out of sessions, or at petty sessions, to omit such convictions, so generally, that in many cases not a tenth part, perhaps not a twentieth part of the actual number of convictions which have led to imprisonment and its pernicious consequences have been sent to the clerks of the peace to be "recorded". A list, therefore, from his files will not give anything like an approximation to the truth of the case.'[19] If Hunt was right about the under-recording of convictions for game laws offences, then the true figure must have been extremely disturbing. He went on to make a sensible proposal for reform. 'I would therefore humbly venture to recommend to you, to procure returns from all the jailers and keepers of houses of corrections in England &c. of the prisoners actually placed in their custody for offences againt the game laws.'

In view of the fact that Hunt's name had several times come to the notice of the Home Secretary, it was scarcely surprising that he should have been asked to give evidence to the Select Committee on Criminal Commitments and Convictions later in the year. It was Lord John Russell who had urged that such a committee be set up, and who was appointed chairman. Perhaps it was he who also suggested that his father's former secretary should give evidence.

In 1828 Hunt received praise from Sir Richard Phillips, one of several publishers imprisoned years earlier for selling Tom Paine's *The Rights of Man.* Phillips published an account of his *Personal Tour,*[20] and wrote, 'I learnt from Mr. Bailey (the Mayor) that the most influential person in Bedford was the Rev. Dr. Hunt, a town and county magistrate, and a clergyman, who possessed various clerical promotions, and the patronage of the Bedford family ...... in him I found nothing of narrow-mindedness or bigotry.'

Reading the many documents prepared by Hunt over the years one gets the impression that his great concern for prisoners lessened after he attained his sixtieth birthday. On 30 April 1832 he wrote a report on behalf of the visiting justices which indicates a hardening of attitude, even though some of the sentiments expressed had been felt by Hunt in earlier times. 'The Visiting Justices have observed with much regret that convicted prisoners are frequently recommitted for minor offences; and they are inclined to attribute this lamentable circumstance (among other causes) to their feeling little if any dread at the thought of being sent again to such state of social intercourse, diet and labour as they find in the houses of correction for this county. The undersigned therefore call the serious attention of their brother justices, in session assembled, to this great evil; and to devise or to adopt some efficacious remedy for it.'[21] Hunt added; 'In no class of delinquents is there any effectual hindrance during the daytime to their perpetually conversing and joking with each other, whether on the treadwheel or during the suspension of work in the relays, or during mealtimes, and the prisoners who are not sentenced to hard labour can even amuse themselves by games of chance, using pebbles or beans on cheque tables marked on their benches or on the ground. And it has often been said that young and inexperienced convicts have been taught by old offenders in the Bedfordshire houses of correction to make snares, and to set them with greater skill, and to commit crimes with greater cunning, than if they had never been sent to prison.'

After this report the discipline in the institutions was considerably tightened up, and T.C. Higgins, one of the visiting justices, later made it clear to a House of Lords Select Committee that Hunt was largely responsible for the changes.[22] Hunt paid his last official visit to the jail on 14 August 1834, although he did not retire from Bedford until the following year. His twenty year interest in the prisoners of the county had been truly remarkable.

1.   *The Parish and the County,* London: Cass, 1963 (reprint), p. 350.
2.   June 1979, p. 748.
3.   *Beds C.R.O.* W 1/360/1. The Whitbread correspondence is quoted by kind permission of Samuel Charles Whitbread Esq.
4.   See, 'Then a Soldier, Unwillingly to School', p.77 *infra.*
5.   Grant, chapter 11.
6.   W 1/2049 and 2050.
7.   QSR 1818/623.
8.   CRT 150/93.
9.   H. G. Bennet, *A Letter to Viscount Sidmouth,* 1818.
10. See, Stockdale, 1977, p. 115 ff.
11. *Parliamentary Papers,* 1821, Vol. 21.
12. QSM 1820/51.
13. Second Report of the Prison Inspectors for the Home District, *Parliamentary Papers,* 1837, Vol. 32.
14. H/WS 1644.
15. *B. L.* Add. Mss. 40,363 f. 100.
16. H/WS 1313 and 1646: letter to Peel, 23 March 1824, referred to above.
17. QSR 1824/137.
18. QGR 4, QSS 4, CRT 180/126.
19. *P.R.O.* HO 52/4.
20. In the County Record Office, but hidden in a volume bearing the title *Beds. Elections Vol. 2,* Z 231/7/2.
21. QGR 4.
22. See, Stockdale, 1977, p. 135.

HUNT AS AN EXPERT WITNESS

Hunt gave evidence to three Parliamentary Select Committees. The first occasion, as we have seen, was in 1816 when he gave evidence to the Members who were considering the purchase of the Elgin Marbles for the nation. Hunt then gave evidence as a witness of fact, rather than as an expert witness. He clearly was an expert on the topic of the Marbles, but he was not asked to give evidence as such, but merely as a man who had personal knowledge of their provenance. It was quite different on the two subsequent occasions when Hunt gave evidence in Westminster. On both of those he was clearly being asked to give evidence as someone with extensive knowledge of an expert nature, whose views as an expert were worth hearing.

On 7 April 1824 Hunt appeared before the Select Committee on Labourers' Wages, with Lord John Russell in the chair.[1] At the outset he made it clear that his presence in Bedford made not only for extra work in connection with the prison, but also with the administration of the poor law. 'Being the only county magistrate residing in the town of Bedford', he pointed out, 'perhaps I have had more applications from the labouring poor in the adjoining parishes than falls to the lot of many of my colleagues in the commission of the peace'. One of his next answers graphically illustrated the distress caused by poverty in the county. 'I believe that the rate of payment of labourers has been reduced so low of late years, that it is impossible for a labourer who is married and has a family, with the greatest energy, assiduity and economy on the part of himself and his wife, to support his family without aid from the parish rates.' When he stated that the usual wage for a single man was five shillings a week or even less, he was asked about such a man's ability to put money aside. Hunt answered, 'I do not think that an unmarried labourer in Bedfordshire is in a situation to lay by anything from his earnings. I would say it is almost impossible for him to support life on his actual wages, if he has lodgings or medicines to pay for, in addition to the expense of food and clothing.'

There followed a telling series of questions and answers about the lot of the married labourer. 'What is the course which a labourer takes to increase his income or wages when he marries and has a family?'

'He applies to the overseer of the parish for assistance, and that assistance in general is doled out in so limited a way that very few labourers marry voluntarily.'

'Do you suppose that the greater proportion of labourers with a family receive assistance from the poor rate in Bedfordshire?'

'I believe that almost every labourer's family that consists of more than himself and his wife and one child has either perpetual or occasional relief from the overseers, either in weekly allowance, or by occasional aid afforded to him either in shoes, clothes or money; and all extraordinary occurrences in such a man's family are paid by the parish, such as attending his wife in labour, or the visitation of sickness. On such occurrences he must apply to the salaried parish apothecary, and when a death occurs in a family, the expense of the funeral is paid out of the poor rates. The principal calculation of the overseer is the amount of what will merely support existence, without any of the extraordinary occurrences that happen in a labourer's family.'

'When a labourer marries there, do you suppose he has no money to pay for any expenses which immediately occur, or are likely soon to occur to him?'

'He has scarcely more than sufficient to pay the marriage fee, and not always that; both the fee and the ring I suspect are sometimes furnished by the parish.' Hunt added, 'Many of them do not marry voluntarily, but the marriage is contracted to avoid the prospect of imprisonment under the bastardy laws.' He went on to explain how he as a magistrate came on the scene. If the parish refused help, the applicant came to the justices. Hunt explained, 'His statement to the magistrate is, that his wages will not enable him to support life, with lodging, washing and other necessary incidental expenses connected with his situation in life. The magistrate in that case recommends the parish officer to grant a small weekly sum, in addition to the earnings of the labourer, as the magistrate has not the power to order the master to pay greater wages, such a sum of money as in addition to his wages will enable him to live. The parish officer then, perhaps, tells the magistrate that he has the option to afford the relief to the applicant, either in money or by placing the dissatisfied labourer in the workhouse, and that he can keep him in the workhouse for three shillings or three shillings and sixpence a week, and the parish be entitled to his labour, and that he is to lodge in the workhouse.' He added that the magistrate would order assistance to be given for a very short period only: until the next petty sessions, where the case could be considered in detail by the bench, rather than by a single justice. Samuel Whitbread's notebooks, recording his adjudications as a single justice out of sessions, contain examples of the kind of decision mentioned by Hunt. For example, on 30 November 1811 Whitbread recorded: 'William Thompson of Haynes wants relief. Witteridge the Haynes overseer present. Thompson sick fourteen days, applied yesterday, overseer bade him wait till the town meeting on Monday, doubting his belonging to Haynes. Reproved the overseer for the delay. Ordered ten shillings to be paid in hand.'[2]

Hunt had very strong views about the connection of poverty with crime and brought in his extensive prison experience. The agricultural labourer, he maintained, 'can scarcely indulge any temporary gratification without having resource to other means than labour; and in counties where game preserves are very numerous, the resource of poaching immediately presents itself to him. If detected he cannot pay the penalty and is consequently sent to prison, where he remains three months, and where he sees other persons not suffering a greater penalty for petty larceny. When he is at length liberated perhaps he goes a step further in delinquency, and he commits an offence that he knows will not be visited more severely than poaching. He breaks open a dove-house, or he steals poultry and other half protected property, and probably he is sent to prison again, and in the end becomes a confirmed depredator or felon; where if he could have gratified an occasional wish for any extra little enjoyment by what he could have saved out of his wages, the first temptation to crime would not have presented itself as strongly to his mind.'

The witness went on to explain how the many surplus labourers in the county were employed and helped financially. Some were employed on farms, where the farmers had assistance with the payment of wages out of public funds. Others were employed by the overseers for parish work only, mainly the repair of roads. Hunt was next asked to explain the system of 'roundsmen'. 'It is sending in rotation to each of the occupiers in the parish those unemployed labourers (who have a parochial settlement in the parish) to work for such farmers, and to have their wages paid, in whole or in part, out of the poor rates ...... They become roundsmen, perhaps, in consequence of their not being so well liked as the other labourers; and by being employed as roundsmen, they become worse still, by the indolent habits they thus acquire.' Michael E. Rose, who quoted this part of Hunt's evidence in his selection of poor law documents, commented, 'The origins of the system are obscure, but it had doubtless been in existence since the eighteenth century, and had been encouraged by statute such as Gilbert's Act, which enjoined on the parish guardian the duty of finding work for the able-bodied unemployed. It was particularly common in winter, when there was little to do on the farms.'[3]

Having described the two plans of either sending men to work on farms or on the roads, Hunt continued, 'And there is a third plan, of having two rates for the support of the labouring population of each parish, viz. one rate for the support of the sick, infirm and impotent poor, and the other is called a labour rate. At a general meeting of parishioners those two rates are made out, by the first of which each landlord in the parish has to pay so much for the general purposes of the relief of the poor, and the other rate is for subdividing the settled labourers of the parish amongst the occupiers.'

Hunt's evidence dealt with many other matters of detail and the printed record runs to more than eight pages. During the course of that evidence he was repeatedly asked for his own views. The reform of the poor law was delayed until after Earl Grey had attained office and until after his government had obtained extensive further evidence from many sources — including Hunt. In the meantime Hunt had been requested to appear before another Select Committee — that on Criminal Commitment and Convictions.[4]

On 30 May and 1 June 1827 the experienced magistrate and prison visitor appeared before the committee. The report of his examination on these two days occupies some sixteen pages of the record. Hunt had personally prepared figures showing the increase in the number of the commitments to prison during the century: he had succeeded in obtaining the figures before his time as a magistrate, from 1801 on. Hunt's most useful return was placed before the committee and the increases commencing with the end of the Napoleonic Wars will be noted. Hunt omitted to inform the committee that one dedicated poacher had made a substantial contribution to the number of game laws conviction. He was James Clare of Woburn, whose first conviction for poaching was in 1804 and who eventually died in prison in 1833 'agreeable to his wishes.'[5]

Thomas Furnivall, Serjeant-Major in the Bedfordshire Militia, standing in front of St. Peter's church, Bedford, c.1790. *Mr. W. S. Knight of Oakley.*

St. Peter's Rectory, Bedford, home of Dr. Philip Hunt, on the sale in 1887 to Bedford School. Sir Richard Phillips, a radical journalist who passed through Bedford in 1828, wrote 'I passed the garden of Dr. Hunt, which, as all taste-ful places ought to be, is protested merely by an green piling.' *Bedfordshire County Record Office*

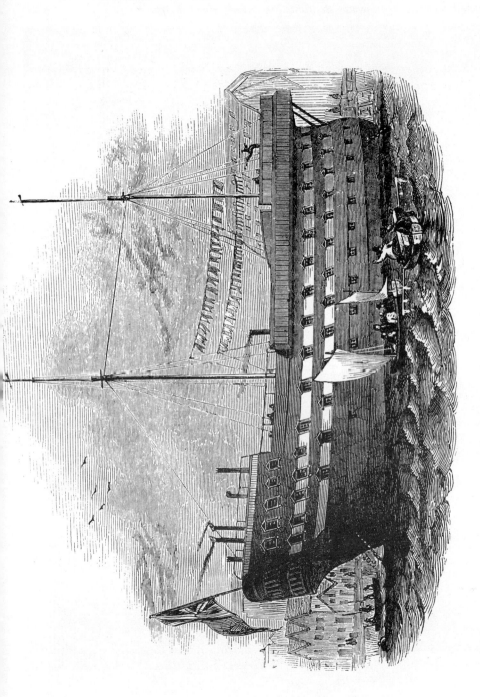

"The Warrior" Convict Hulk, Woolwich. *Illustrated London News Picture Library.*

P.C. 32 (possibly Police Constable Henry Butterworth) photographed by Micklethwaite of Biggleswade. *Bedfordshire County Record Office.*

When he was asked to explain the increase in the number of commitments Hunt reverted to his old theme about the contamination of minor offenders by the more sophisticated criminals they met in prison. He made the additional point, 'there has been a great increase of commitments for small offences owing to the facility with which petty criminals can be convicted before single justices out of sessions ...... I think a great many offences are thus brought to conviction that would not be thought of if they had to go to a more distant or expensive tribunal; the power of summary jurisdiction has been very much extended in latter years.' One can understand that someone might have expected the increase in summary committals possibly to lead to a decrease in crime, so that the next question is not surprising. Hunt was asked, 'Do you think that this circumstance tends to the diminution of crime, or to the increase of crime?' He replied, 'I am afraid to the increase both of criminal commitments and of crime; because a person once sent to prison gets into a course of criminal habits by associating with dissolute persons whom he meets there.' When asked about the effect of better prison discipline, Hunt replied sadly, 'I fear that very little improvement is ever made in the moral habits of a prisoner by even the best forms of prison discipline and instruction that have been yet devised.'

Hunt told the committee about his strong views back in 1818 that a prison should be established for young prisoners convicted of trifling offences only, and was asked what the effect of that new house of correction had been. Regretfully he told the committee, 'Not so great as I could have expected; because the new prison laws that have been enacted since that time have produced the effect of sending to that secondary prison many convicted of crimes at the assizes and sessions, so that the magistrates have no longer the power to keep that prison to the mild purpose for which they originally intended it.' This last answer was a very sad one. The views of Hunt and others who shared his ideas about the separation of different classes of prisoners, had led to the building of the new house of correction. Then the idea of separation had gathered momentum, until Parliament had passed the Prison Acts which made such detailed provision for the separation of classes that Hunt and his colleagues had been forced to use the new house of correction for some old-style villains, for the old jail was not large enough for all the required separate quarters. The good idea had grown to such an extent that it had been partly self-defeating.

The committee asked the witness to list the principal causes of the increase in crime in Bedfordshire. The first three causes given by Hunt were not new, but the fourth was fresh. 'I would say, first, the distress of the agricultural labourer driving him to offences against the game laws, or to committing petty offences; secondly, the effect of the bastardy laws; and thirdly, the facility with which summary convictions take place for petty offences; and perhaps I may also mention the great facility of convicting afforded by associations for the prosecution of hedge breakers and other trespassers and delinquents ...... It occurred to me last week to see a person who had all his legal expenses paid by such an association, for pursuing a hedge breaker, and 28 shillings allowed to him for travelling expenses in having gone from one parish to another in searching for a justice; a sum altogether, I think, that man would not have incurred if his own pocket had been the source from whence it was to be supplied.'

Time and again Hunt gave answers to the committee which correspond closely with those given to similar committees nowadays by enlightened witnesses. 'Do you think', he was asked about the inmates' dread of prison, 'the increased order which has been introduced into jails, cleanliness, and so on, and good food, which is sometimes given there, has in a certain degree tended to decrease that dread?' 'I do not think that prisoners have less dislike of going to jail on those accounts;' the witness replied, 'the deprivation of liberty is what they most dislike.'

So, too, when asked about corporal punishment, Hunt gave some modern answers. 'I am afraid that corporal punishment would degrade the mind even more than imprisonment, or that it would have at least all the bad effects consequent on loss of character.' In answer to a question about private whipping, he replied, 'I think there are very great objections to private punishments.'

Hunt was very interested in education generally and had some comments to make on the link between inadequate education and crime. He was asked, 'You say that the domestic discipline of the children is neglected by their parents;' He replied, 'Yes; from their supposing that the school gives those moral lessons which I fear the school does not give ...... The parents expect from village schools more practical moral discipline than schools so constituted are capable of affording.'

Hunt's answers to questions about poaching are worth repeating. He was asked, 'Are not the poachers somewhat hardened by the belief that the punishment has exceeded the offence?'

'They do generally express themselves as of opinion that the punishment is greater than the offence deserves.'

'And that exasperates them?'

'Yes; and they sometime venture to think they have hardly had a fair trial for such offences, when they have been convicted by strict preservers of game, who have frequently been sufferers.'

'And that no doubt has a bad effect upon their moral character?'

'No doubt it makes them dissatisfied, if they think they have been convicted by a party interested, and sent to prison for what they deem no crime.'

It may well have been these answers of Hunt's — coupled with some remarks about Turkish justice — which inspired Whitbread's friend, Henry Brougham, to make similar comments in his great law reform speech in the House of Commons on 7 February of the following year. Brougham, allowing himself his usual advocate's licence, protested, 'There is not a worse constituted tribunal on the face of the earth, not even that of the Turkish Cadi, than that at which summary convictions on the Game Laws constantly take place; I mean a bench or a brace of sporting justices.'[6] Earlier in his speech Brougham, the future Whig Lord Chancellor, had stated, 'I have very great doubts as to the expediency of making clergymen magistrates ...... My opinion is that a clerical magistrate, in uniting two very excellent and useful characters, pretty generally spoils both.' That criticism could certainly not be fairly made of Philip Hunt.

We have seen that Hunt spent some time at Canterbury, but he died on 17 September 1838 at Aylsham in Norfolk, where he was vicar and where he was looked after by his niece, Fanny Gould. The church there has a wall monument which describes him as 'a powerful preacher, an elegant scholar, an efficient and active magistrate'. After his death letters of tribute flowed in to his niece,[7] but real public acknowledgment of his truly remarkable efforts never came.

1. Parliamentary Papers, 1824, Vol. 6. For Hunt's evidence in its proper context, see Nigel E. Agar. 'The Bedfordshire Farm Worker in the Nineteenth Century'. *B.H.R.S.* Vol. 60, 1981.
2. Alan F. Cirket, 'Samuel Whitbread's Notebooks, 1810-11, 1813-14', *B.H.R.S.* Vol. 50, 1971, p. 73.
3. *The English Poor Law 1780-1930,* Michael E. Rose, Newton Abbot: David & Charles, 1971, p. 56.
4. Parliamentary Papers, 1826-7, Vol. 6.
5. CRT 180/102.
6. Henry Brougham, *Present State of the Law,* London: Henry Colburn, 1828, pp. 39 and 36.
7. Hunt Papers. *The Gentleman's Magazine,* 1838 Vol. 2, p.561, only accorded Hunt a very inadequate obituary.

III
AN APPEAL TO SAMUEL WHITBREAD FROM THE HULKS

On 30 October 1809 Thomas Creevey, Samuel Whitbread's Parliamentary friend and colleague, arrived at Southill to stay for a few days. On 4 November Creevey wrote in his journal: 'We leave Whitbread's for London, having spent a very happy time at Southill, and with a most firm conviction that Whitbread — though rough in manners — though entirely destitute of all taste or talent for conversation, and though apparently almost tyrannical in his deportment to his inferiors — is a man of the very strictest integrity, with the most generous, kind and feeling heart.'[1] In the next essay we shall be looking at some of Whitbread's conduct as a militia colonel, conduct which might loosely be described as 'almost tyrannical', but for the present we shall be concerned with the characteristic which probably predominated throughout his career, 'the most generous, kind and feeling heart'. In particular, we shall be looking at an appeal which was made to that heart shortly before Creevey's visit.

Throughout his career as a politician Whitbread showed a concern for the underdog, whether the instant problem was one of low wages, lack of educational opportunities, or some other social problem. He even took up the cudgels on behalf of that oppressed wife, the Princess of Wales. Inevitably he was approached for help by different sufferers, including prisoners. Whitbread was interested in prisoners in the county jail, in those transferred to the hulks and in those transported to New South Wales. When Sir Samuel Romilly suggested that a national penitentiary should be built to replace the hulks, he was warmly supported by Whitbread.[2]

On 18 July 1810 Joseph Boneham of Turvey wrote a farewell letter to his wife from '*Indian*, Spithead, bound for New South Wales'. The departing prisoner wrote, 'I hope you will endeavour to see Mr. Whitbread and remind him of me.'[3]

William Fennell wrote to Whitbread on 8 April 1811 informing him that he was aged 74, and had been on the *Zealand* hulk at Sheerness for four years — ever since the Bedford Assizes of March 1807. His story was that he had been found sleeping in an outhouse and had been fined a shilling by the court. Then someone had passed some information to the judge who had promptly varied the sentence to seven years' transportation.[4] Whatever the truth of the matter, like many other prisoners sentenced to be transported, Fennell was left to rot for some years on one of the terrible hulks, so well described by W. Branch Johnson.[5] He was only eventually transported in July 1812.[6]

Whether Whitbread was able to do anything for either of these two men is not clear, but he retained their letters, so presumably interested himself in their plight. Whitbread may have been partly inspired by the reflection that he was a cousin of the great John Howard, and partly by his own father's good example. In 1789, the year in which the first Bedfordshire prisoners were transported to New South Wales, Samuel Whitbread the Elder received a letter from John Moore Howard, the Bedford jailer (no relation of the reformer) about a prisoner not unlike Fennell. It read:

'I thought it my duty to inform you of having this day received the Secretary's order to remove all the convicts on board the hulks lying at Langston Harbour. As the order is general for all the male convicts, cannot omit poor old Wm. Goodman, consequently the old man must go without your kind interference with the Secretary. He has experienced your goodness twice before which has prevented his going abroad: and I trust in God he may the third time, hoping his age and good behaviour whilst in prison will plead for his not leaving his native country in his advanced age, he having been a prisoner confined within these walls seven years the 18th. of next month. The favour of your answer by Sunday's post, as I must be in Town on Monday with the convicts, will much oblige.'[7]

Whitbread sent the letter on to Evan Nepean, the Under-Secretary at the Home Office, with a covering note which probably succeeded in getting relief for the old prisoner. 'Mr. Whitbread presents his compliments to Mr. Nepean, received the inclosed today from Bedford and begs the favour of Mr. N. to order Goodman to be sent back to Bedford. Mr. W. has written to the jailer to wait upon Mr. Nepean on Tuesday morning and is very sorry to be troublesome; but the poor wretch's time will be out in March and he is 76 years of age.'

In April 1809 Whitbread asked a question in the House of Commons about New South Wales. The newspaper account of this matter led to his being sent documents about the colony by Thomas Wheldale.[8] It may also have been that report of the proceedings in Parliament which led to Whitbread receiving papers asking him to intervene on behalf of William John Speed, 'late Lieut. Colonel of the St. Vincent Rangers, sentenced to transportation for seven years for having married a second wife seven years after his first wife had totally deserted him and three children she had by him and lived for seventeen years in a state of prostitution with other men'.[9]

Speed had been in custody, awaiting trial at the Surrey Assizes in March 1809, for some seven months. According to Speed's later appeal to the Secretary of State he 'suffered severely from the cold and draught of the cell at Horsemonger Lane', and the surgeon there certified that he suffered from rheumatism.[10]

Speed's 'Case as far as relates to the conduct he has experienced from John Capper Esq., Head Clerk in the office of the Secretary of State for the Home Department', was contained in a truly remarkable document, which bore the dateline 'Woolwich, 11 July 1809' and read as follows:

'When Mr. Speed was convicted, had received sentence and was hurried off on board the hulks at Woolwich, he wrote to his friends to petition and intercede with the Secretary of State for mercy — Mr. Speed has sufficient proofs of the injustice of his sentence and the *private* charges made against him, of ill-treatment of his first wife and her children, not only from the evidence of most respectable persons, but letters of her own, and of his children — these letters Mr. Speed wished to be perused by Mr. Capper, having heard that he (Mr. Capper) bore the character of a humane, honourable and benevolent man. For this purpose Mr. Speed sent his last wife (with whom he has lived nine years and had four children by, two of which are now living), with those papers to Mr. Capper, accompanied by a petition to be presented to the Secretary of State praying, that if no other mitigation of the sentence could be granted, Mr. Speed might be permitted to transport himself.

'Mr. Capper pretends to have been struck with the appearance of Mrs. Speed on his first seeing her, and determined from that moment to possess her, if by any possible scheme it could be accomplished. (It may be proper to observe that Mr. Capper has a sister, a widow named Ward, who lets lodgings in Marsham Street, Westminster, with whom a lady and her daughter, friends of Mrs. Ward, lodge.) Mr. Capper at the first interview desired Mrs. Speed to call again in a day or two, and he would see what could be done; here it was contrived that Mrs. Ward (the sister) was to be introduced to Mrs. Speed. When Mrs. Speed called upon Mr. Capper at the time appointed, he told her he was afraid nothing could be done for Mr. Speed, as the Judge who tried him pointedly opposed it. (This answer, Mr. Speed finds, was given by Mr. Capper to Sir Walter James, Admiral Bentick, Mr. Hatsell, and other friends who interested themselves on the subject.)

'Mrs. Speed represented to Mr. Capper the distressing situation she must be in, with her two children totally dependent upon Mr. Speed for support, if he should be sent out of the country leaving her behind, and asked Mr. Capper if herself and the children would not be allowed to go out with Mr. Speed. Mr. Capper said that could most certainly not be allowed, and as to herself, there was no doubt she would meet with friends who would be happy to take care of her. Mr. Capper told her, if it could be even permitted her to accompany Mr. Speed, her situation would be dreadful, as she would certainly be the *only female* on board the ship, and New South Wales was such a miserable place, it was *shocking for any* decent woman to go to it.

'Mr. Capper now employed his sister to work upon the feelings of Mrs. Speed by constantly presenting the dangers of the voyage and the length of it, which he said could not be less than nine months, with many other circumstances tending to inspire a dreadful idea of the dangers into the mind of Mrs. Speed, and when she (Mrs. Ward) conceived she had alarmed her, said Mr. Capper thought *her the most charming woman he had ever seen*, and such a woman *as he should be happy to pass his life with* — that he had never had a child by any woman, and if he was *to have a child, he should adore the woman who bore it.* Here Mrs. Speed observed to Mrs. Ward that she thought she was going too far to talk to a married woman in that way (as she certainly considered herself most religiously so to Mr. Speed, and would never be brought to forsake the father of her children, let his situation be what it might; that she had shared the dangers of the seas, the horrors of a French prison, and other perils with him, and was determined to be the partner of his fate as long as they both should live).'

Before continuing with the Case it might be as well to consider some of the basic facts. It was undoubtedly true that John Henry Capper held a clerk's position, and that he wielded enormous power, particularly after his promotion to superintendent rank in 1815. This is what A.G.L. Shaw, the principal historian of transportation, had to say about Capper after his promotion: 'Capper decided who should be transported and who kept on board, though it seems strange that this decision should rest not with the Secretary of State, but with the Superintendent, who was consequently the · man to ask for favours. For example, in 1817, William Lamb (later Lord Melbourne) asked Capper for favour towards the *brother* of one of his servants; since the latter was a "most meritorious character", perhaps the former, who was a first offender, might "merit indulgence". Capper reported that the culprit's conduct was good and agreed to "recommend him for release at the end of the year when half of his sentence has expired".'[11]

Capper would presumably not have been promoted in 1815 — the year of Whitbread's suicide — had he not had a reasonable reputation with the Home Secretary. He certainly managed to impress Whitbread's friend and fellow Member of Parliament, H.G. Bennet (who was Lord William Russell's son-in-law). In 1819 Bennet published an open letter to Lord Sidmouth, the Home Secretary, in which he praised Capper extravagantly after a visit to the hulks. 'Having however visited all these establishments, it is my duty to say that no one can engage in that painful task without finding at every step something to praise in the good sense, humanity, and attention of that valuable public servant.'[12]

Three years after Speed's appeal to Whitbread, Capper was to give evidence to the Select Committee on Transportation. He was asked, 'If a convict be married, is any facility afforded to his wife to accompany him if she should choose?' Capper replied, 'It was formerly attended to, but strong objections have arisen on the part of the Transport Board in allowing them at all events to accompany them; in some instances we have allowed them to follow in other ships ...... We should not allow a female to go out whose husband was under a seven years' transportation; in those cases where they are under a sentence of transportation for life, we have endeavoured to send them out, and we have in most cases done it.'[13] *If* this evidence was correct — then Capper was at any rate telling Mrs. Speed the truth about the impossibility of her accompanying her husband. However, later passages in the papers cast doubt on this statement of his.

Speed's Case against Capper continued: 'Mrs. Speed had left letters and papers favourable to Mr. Speed in the hands of Mr. Capper, to be laid before Lord Liverpool, when on Mrs. Speed calling at the Secretary of State's office on 23 May, Mr. Capper, after speaking on the subject, said to her, "If you will promise not to go out to the West Indies with Mr. Speed, should I obtain permission to transport himself, I will procure the papers to be laid before the judge and try what I can do".' Speed's reference to the West Indies, where he had served as a soldier, was clearly a slip of the pen for New South Wales. Speed went on, 'Mr. Speed consulted with and showed these letters to Captain Reed, the Commander of the Hulks (whose humane and benevolent conduct will ever be felt with the most sincere gratitude by Mr. Speed), when Captain Reed expressed his astonishment at Mr. Capper's conduct, and could not have supposed him capable of so base an action, he also informed Mr. Speed that several women had accompanied their husbands in the last ship, and also that Government had been so very indulgent that four women (wives of convicts) for whom there was not room in the ship with their husbands, had been permitted to go in the women convict ship, and the husbands also permitted to go out in that ship, Captain Reed himself having taken them on board.' It is of interest to note that only a female convict ship *arrived* in New South Wales in 1809, and no male one.[14]

Speed's account turned to his last days in England. 'A few days before the embarkation of the convicts from the hulks on board the transport, Captain Reed was at the Secretary of State's office, where he saw Mr. Capper who asked him if Speed was reconciled to his fate. Captain Reed answered he believed he was, and had prepared for the voyage. Mr. Capper said he had heard *she* (meaning Mrs. Speed) was going with him, was it true? Captain Reed replied he believed it was, for that he had seen letters which stated an order having been given by the Transport Board for her and the children being received on board the ship in which Mr. Speed was to go. Mr. Capper asked if he knew by what means or interest that order had been obtained. Captain Reed answered he did not know, but that he had seen a letter from Sir Rupert George to Mrs. Speed which mentioned it, and which letter appeared to be written in a friendly style. Mr. Capper in a violent rage declared she should not go, that the ship was not in the class of common transport but taken up for a particular service, that the Transport Board had no right or power to give such an order, and by God, it should be enquired into. Captain Reed the next day informed Mr. Speed of the conversation, saying that he considered Mr. Capper's conduct so scandalous, he felt himself bound in honour to acquaint Mr. Speed with it.'

The appeal from Speed doubtless put Whitbread in a dilemma. If Capper was as powerful and as obnoxious as the one-sided evidence indicated, then he might make matters worse for the prisoner in his power. On the other hand, Whitbread would have felt obliged to do something about such an impassioned plea, so full of details which had the ring of truth. Had there been ample time, no doubt Whitbread could and would have approached Captain Reed. Speed had indicated that one member of the government, Lord Liverpool, might have been shown some of the documents in the case, so it made sense for Whitbread, an opposition member, to contact him also. Whitbread left no account of what happened, but an anguished letter from Speed continued his tale of woe. It came from Sydney, New South Wales and was dated 2 May 1810, Speed having left the Thames on 31 July 1809.[15]

'When I last took the liberty of addressing myself to you on the subject of Mr. Capper's conduct, I find you sent my letter and statements to Lord Liverpool, in consequence of which Mr. Capper was alarmed. He sent his sister (Mrs. Ward of Marsham St., Westminster) to Mrs. Speed, begging for God's sake she would go to the Secretary of State's Office and soften off the charges I had made, as a mother and sister dependent solely on Mr. Capper for maintenance. Her going had the effect of stopping an enquiry which must have brought down censure on Mr. Capper, but his conduct then became more villainous, as the statements I take the liberty of enclosing will evince, nor should I even have noticed that, as I had succeeded in procuring a passage for my wife and children, but that on my arrival here I find Mr. Capper has written to some persons here vilifying my character, by which conduct I am deprived of that respect and attention I should from the recommendation of others experience until I can make it appear Mr. Capper's charges are false and malicious.'

This last paragraph of Speed's letter is most interesting. It would seem from this that Mrs. Speed did indeed put in a word for the dastardly Capper. A possible explanation for this is that her husband was still in the civil servant's clutches, and that she was prepared to do anything, other than surrender her honour (as they say), in order to help Speed. The other point to note is that Speed was successful in securing a passage for his family, despite Capper's hostility, which suggests that, whilst he may have been powerful, he was not all-powerful. It also confirms Speed's assertions to Whitbread about having important friends who could help him. There is nothing in this letter to suggest that the family did not succeed in embarking on the same ship, so the Speeds possibly set sail together.

Speed continued: 'To prove the facts stated in the inclosure, Mr. Reed (who commands the hulks at Woolwich) and his clerk Mr. Brown may be called upon, as also Mr. Radcliffe, who lodges with Mrs. Ward (Mr. Capper's sister), as also Mrs. Ward herself, and the letters I inclosed to Lord Liverpool will prove that part of the charge.

'I well know but for Mr. Capper's scandalous exertion of the influence which his situation gives him, I should not have been sent out to this place, as I had the most respectable persons applying for a remission of my sentence, and if inquiry should be made, it will be found it is Mr. Capper's custom to debauch the wives and sisters of unhappy persons whose sentence induces the poor women to apply to him, and then send the men out here that no enquiry may be made. It is a well known fact that three brothers, notorious offenders, were on board the *Retribution* hulk when I was — one (if not two) had been sentenced to transportation before, but pardoned by the influence of Mr. Capper, and he actually sent a message to them before I left the ship that one (if not all three) should be pardoned before Christmas. It may be necessary here to explain that the mother and aunt of these men keep a bawdy-house in Wych Street, where Mr. Capper is a constant visitor.

'Trusting in your philanthropy and as a promoter of justice, I take the liberty of thus submitting my case as it is certainly a perversion of justice if a man for a most trifling offence, and where every circumstance is favourable to him, should be sent to this wretched place whose every inhabitant (almost) is a thief, when notorious and professed thieves are let loose upon the public to renew their depradations because they may have a sister or a relative who can administer to the lewd pleasures of Mr. Capper. Thus situated I hope I shall meet your pardon for the liberty I now take as I may not be able to return to England within the time limited by law for commencing prosecutions after the fact committed.'

Speed's account of his matrimonial difficulties was rather different from that which was given to the Secretary of State by his trial judge, Sir Archibald MacDonald.[16] Sir Archibald, a former Attorney General, reported on 20 May 1809 that he had tried Speed at the Surrey Assizes in March for bigamy. Speed's first marriage was to Sarah Wilson at Furneaux Pelham in Hertfordshire in 1785, and that lady was still alive when he went through a second, bigamous, ceremony with Ann Thorn in 1799. The first Mrs. Speed had apparently suffered from some mental illness and had been under the care of Francis Willis, the doctor who had treated George III for what was thought to be madness, but may have been porphyria. (The royal patient described Dr. Willis as 'that ugly old fumbling fellow'.)

According to the judge the only defence put forward by Speed at his trial was that he had thought he was entitled to remarry, as he had been involved in litigation before Chief Justice Kenyon who had said during the course of the case, that 'he and his wife were as free as air — as free as if they had never been married'. Speed's trial judge added the comment, 'It appears to me impossible that a man who has received the education and kept the company which a Lieutenant Colonel in the army must be presumed to have done, could be ignorant of the necessity of obtaining an Act of Parliament to enable him to marry another wife when the first is living'. In the circumstances he had felt obliged to 'make an example' of the accused by passing the sentence of transportation for seven years.

In parenthesis it may be noted that Sir Archibald MacDonald made some interesting comments in his report about the varying degrees of seriousness of bigamy offences. The case which he thought 'calls for great lenity' was that 'where the parish officers give the father of a child, which if born alive will be a bastard chargeable to the parish, the choice of the jail or the altar. He generally prefers the latter. The parties see no more of each other, and the parties frequently marry other persons'. As we have seen, Philip Hunt had spoken about similar occasions where 'the marriage is contracted to avoid imprisonment under the bastardy laws'.[17]

We do not know what happened to Speed in Australia. Some transported convicts had a miserable time out there, but others did quite well for themselves, as various letters home showed.[18] In 1827 Philip Hunt was to tell a Select Committee chaired by his former charge, Lord John Russell, 'I believe that latterly offenders have not been afraid of a sentence that leads really to transportation ...... I saw a letter from a convict in New South Wales addressed to a friend in the village where he had lived in Bedfordshire, stating that he was the owner of a considerable estate.'[19]

Four years later, Thomas Potter Macqueen of Ridgmont, grandson of Thomas Potter of the 1757 Militia Act fame, told Members of Parliament that he considered the condition of the convict labourer in New South Wales to be infinitely superior to that of the labourer in this country. He spoke with authority as he was a landowner in the colony, and he added, 'I have found from my own experience as a magistrate that many persons have asked what extent of crime would ensure their transportation.'[20]

A later Select Committee, on which Lord John Russell also served, was told by the penal reformer, Captain Alexander Maconochie, 'The condition of a transported convict is a mere lottery; it may and does range between the extremes of comfort and misery; no single case can be looked upon as a type of the whole system.'[21]

It is quite possible that Speed's friends in London were able to help him once he got out to Australia, and that his military and other skills stood him in good stead, and enabled him to recover from the barbarous treatment he had received at the hands of the State and its servant, John Henry Capper.

Capper may have deserved an early sticky end, but such is life that he had a long career in the public service. Branch Johnson called Chapter Ten of his book on the hulks 'The Reign of J.H. Capper'. That miserable reign lasted until 1847, when the publication of a report by Captain William John Williams (a Prison Inspector), on the state of the hulks, finally exposed Capper, although for his neglect rather than for sexual improprieties. Williams reported, 'The infirmities of age and ill-health of Mr. J.H. Capper have prevented me from obtaining from him personally explanations upon the many points in which he is involved in this inquiry'. Capper's failure to co-operate was not enough to save him, and he was duly pensioned off, but the last hulk was only disposed of ten years later, when fire gutted the *Defence*.[22] It is impossible to get anything like an accurate picture of what really happened under Capper's rule. A recent researcher had made the following significant comment: 'Much of the evidence for the state of the hulks is taken from documents dated 1847 and onwards, because until that date, when the Home Office took a much closer control over the administration of the hulks, they had been in the hands of Henry John Capper, who kept scant records.'[23] In fairness to Capper one should also add that it would be unwise to assume that the facts which Speed recounted to Whitbread were accurate, for Speed's own appeal to Lord Liverpool contains many inconsistencies which make it difficult to decide where the truth lies.[24]

Captain Williams was closely concerned with Bedford prison after exposing Capper. In July 1846 Lord John Russell became Prime Minister, with Sir George Grey (Whitbread's nephew) as his Home Secretary. Grey re-organised the Prison Inspectorate and placed Bedford prison in the Midland and Eastern District under Captain Williams, who made a significant contribution to the improvement of the lot of Bedfordshire prisoners.

1. H. Maxwell, *The Creevey Papers*, London: John Murray, 1912, p. 110.
2. Sidney and Beatrice Webb, *English Prisons under Local Government*, London: Cass (reprint), 1963, p. 47.
3. W 1/4947.
4. W 1/5002.
5. W. Branch Johnson, *The English Prison Hulks*, rev. ed., Chichester: Phillimore, 1970.
6. *P.R.O.* HO 7 p. 3.
7. *P.R.O.* HO 42/15 f. 220; for John Moore Howard see, Eric Stockdale, 'The Last of the Family of Gaolers', *Bedfordshire Magazine*, Vol. 14, 1974, p. 255.
8. W 1/4984-7.
9. W 1/4944.
10. *P.R.O.* HO 47/41; *Surrey C.R.O.* QS2/5/1809 Ep/45, 46.

11. A. G. L. Shaw, *Convicts and the Colonies,* London: Faber, 1966, p. 137.
12. H. G. Bennet, *A Letter to Viscount Sidmouth,* London 1819, p. 13.
13. Select Committee on Transportation Report, Parl. Papers, 1812, Vol. 2.
14. A. G. L. Shaw, p. 364.
15. W 1/4945; *P.R.O.* HO 9/4 and T 38/335.
16. *P.R.O.* HO 47/41.
17. See also, Alan F. Cirket, 'Samuel Whitbread's Notebooks, 1810-11, 1813-14', *B.H.R.S.* Vol. 50, 1971, p. 16.
18. A. Underwood, 'Some Letters from Beds. Prisoners in Australia, 1842-86', *B.H.R.S.* Vol. 40, p. 228; H. W. Foster, 'Letters of Richard Dillingham, Convict', *B.H.R.S.* Vol. 49, p. 171.
19. Select Committee on Criminal Commitments and Convictions, Parl. Papers, 1826-27, Vol. 6.
20. Select Committee on Secondary Punishments, Parl. Papers, 1831, Vol. 7.
21. Select Committee on Transportation, Parl. Papers, 1838, Vol. 22.
22. W. Branch Johnson, pp. 184, 198.
23. M. Heather Tomlinson, 'Penal Servitude 1846-1865: A System in Evolution', in Victor Bailey (ed.) *Policing and Punishment in Nineteenth Century Britain,* London: Croom Helm, 1981, p. 144 n. 9.
24. *P.R.O.* HO 47/41.

IV
THEN A SOLDIER, UNWILLINGLY TO SCHOOL

In 1809 there were two regiments of the Bedfordshire Local Militia, ready to repulse Napoleon. Samuel Whitbread commanded the First with the rank of Lieutenant-Colonel, and Lord St. John the Second. Whitbread's adjutant was Lieutenant Charles Bailey, and one of the sergeants serving under them both was Richard Warden, a local carpenter. The non-commissioned officers of the regiment, including Warden, were only required to be full-time soldiers for one month in the year, when the regiment was embodied, but during the remainder of the year they received some pay, and were obliged to make themselves available for drill periods. The non-commissioned officers were from time to time required to write down orders, and so Colonel Whitbread, like some of his militia colleagues, decided to raise the standard of literacy in his unit, by requiring the sergeants and corporals to go to evening classes. Whitbread in the House of Commons had been a keen supporter of the idea of universal education, and so one can readily understand his enthusiasm for the further education of the more important members of his regiment.

The news of the idea of evening classes was broken to the non-commissioned officers by Lieutenant Bailey one day in November 1809, when they were all assembled in the Race Meadow, off the Ampthill Road. Bailey told his part-time military subordinates that their colonel expected them to attend classes every evening of the week so that their ability to read and write might be improved. Their teacher was to be their own Sergeant-Major, Thomas Warner, and each pupil was to have the privilege of paying eightpence a week for tuition, or, as one sergeant later put it, 'to find fire and candle, and to pay the schoolmaster'. In practice, no-one was ever required to make any payment.[1]

Understandably some of the militiamen resented being ordered to go to school at their own expense. What made the whole thing worse for some was that they were mocked by the children who learned about their return to school. A hoary old corporal called Dickens Prigmore, who had 'been a soldier going on twenty-one years', and who said that whilst his fingers were a little too stiff for a pen, 'they are lissom enough for a firelock', found that the children laughed at him and his colleagues. Some of the more independently minded of the soldiers decided to play truant, and for that offence seven were summoned to attend a special parade in the yard of the *Swan* in Bedford on Friday 1 December 1809. They were called into the inn one at a time by Sergeant-Major Warner, the schoolmaster, where they had an opportunity of explaining themselves to Colonel Whitbread, who was attended by Lieutenant Bailey.

Sergeant Richard Warden was duly wheeled in before his commanding officer, and begged pardon for his failure to attend school. He gave no hint of rebellion, and did not suggest that the school requirement was illegal or unjust, nor did he say that he would not attend school in future. In short, he submitted quietly, and his apology was accepted. That was the end of the matter as far as Colonel Whitbread was concerned. Warden went back into the inn yard and heard one of his truant colleagues, Sergeant John Cooper, called in for the second time. According to the later evidence of the senior sergeant in the regiment, Thomas Smith, Warden called out to Cooper, 'Damn your eyes, Jack, don't give up — don't yield — don't go to school, for I'll be damned if I do.' Smith reacted at once, warning Warden, 'By God Almighty, such language as that is enough to make the men mutiny.' Warden replied that he did not care about that. Cooper would not apologise to Whitbread and was despatched to the town jail to await a regimental court martial on the following Tuesday.

Next morning, Saturday 2 December, the adjutant asked Smith for an account of what had happened in the yard, and the sergeant recounted what Warden had said. Cooper and other soldiers later said they had not heard a single word from Warden; had Smith had a similar 'lapse of memory', there would have been no subsequent litigation, but as luck would have it, he decided to answer his officer honestly, and the latter reacted extravagantly.

The adjutant sent for Warden to come to his own yard and put it to him that he had used words which might have led to a mutiny. Warden denied saying anything inflammatory. Bailey decided his conduct was so grave that he ordered Warden to be detained until he could be brought before Whitbread, who had left town. As the soldiers were part-timers only, the actual business of incarceration was not at all straightforward. Bailey first of all ordered Sergeant Lavender to draw his sword and to guard the miscreant. Then he ordered Corporal Tompkins, another truant, who thought the sergeant-major to be 'a pretty midlingish scholar' only, but who had got away with begging the colonel's pardon, to fetch a file of corporals. Tompkins passed the order on to Sergeant Smith, who was not in uniform, but who responded promptly. He found old Dickens Prigmore working 'at Mr. Rawlin's cellar' and there, according to the worthy corporal, 'He ordered me to go home and put my regimentals on and have my firelock; which it was about twenty minutes before ten when he ordered me, and I believe I was about thirty minutes in putting my regimentals on and getting to the adjutant's yard.' It took the sergeant rather longer to climb into his uniform and get back to the yard, complete with halbert. There he found Warden still being guarded by Lavender and his sword. The adjutant and sergeant-major came out and, in Prigmore's words, 'The adjutant said, "Warden, you have done enough to be shot; Sergeant Smith, take this man, Warden, to jail, and tell Castleman that he is to be locked up, and he ain't to go nigh Cooper, but to be locked up, live on bread and water, and nobody to go nigh him" '.

Warden was duly marched off to the little town jail on the north side of the town. Sergeant Smith led the way, followed by the prisoner and then the two armed corporals, Prigmore and Thomas Barnes. They marched across the bridge, then past St. Paul's church and the courthouse. When they arrived at the jail, Castleman the jailer was out, but Mrs. Castleman who was minding the business in the best tradition of Bedford jailers' wives, admitted them all. Warden was duly locked up in a cell and the escort departed.

Adjutant Bailey informed Colonel Whitbread as soon as he could, and on Monday, 4 December, the prisoner was produced before his commanding officer, where he denied the allegations made against him once more. Whitbread decided that the matter was too serious for a mere regimental court-martial, such as the one he had ordered for Cooper, and ordered that Warden be taken back to jail to await a general court-martial for his mutinous words. On the next day Whitbread wrote to General Henry Pigot, 'I am exceedingly sorry to be under the necessity of troubling you on such an occasion; but I must request the favour of you to give directions for assembling a general court-martial upon Sergeant Warden, of the first regiment of Bedfordshire Local Militia, confined upon the charge of exciting disobedience and mutiny. Your early attention to this application will much oblige.'

On 9 December Warden wrote to Whitbread to request a copy of the charges which were to be laid before the court-martial, and on 11 December the general sent a similar request. In his letter the general informed Whitbread, 'I have written to the adjutant-general by this post on the subject of assembling a general court-martial', but on 30 December he reported a snag. 'I have the honour to inform you that the Commander in Chief approves of my convening a General Court-Martial, for the trial of Sergeant Richard Warden, but there not being a sufficient number of militia corps in my district, I have written to the Adjutant-General on the subject, and on receiving his answer, I will let you know where the Court Martial will assemble.' On 2 January 1810 the general informed the colonel that the trial would be held at Norman Cross in Leicestershire, where many thousands of prisoners of war were guarded by large numbers of militiamen. The warrant for holding the trial, under the King's Sign Manual, was dated 12 January, and appointed Lieutenant-Colonel Richard Gilpin, of the Bedfordshire Regiment of Militia, to be President. The court-martial took place on 30 and 31 January, and Warden was acquitted. Six of his fellow soldiers gave evidence for him, but the acquittal was probably attributable in part to the thirteen members of the court sensibly treating the whole affair as a storm in a teacup. The acquittal was not the end of the matter for Warden, for that result had first to be confirmed by higher authority. It was only on 11 March that the acquittal was approved and Warden completely freed. We must go back to December to see how much the wretched carpenter had been deprived of his freedom in the preceding fourteen weeks.

For the first three days of his imprisonment in the town jail Warden had the company of Cooper, but on the Tuesday Cooper was sentenced by the regimental court-martial to be reduced to the ranks for his insubordination, and so did not return to custody. On the same day Warden was joined by an equally dangerous criminal: John Pennyfather, an apprentice who had been imprisoned as a result of 'some difference' with his master, which was resolved by his release after two weeks on his agreeing to pay a sum of money to the master. He and Warden usually slept in the same bed to keep warm. Pennyfather later explained, 'Over the door was iron bars, and the wind came in unaccountably; the wind came in to our heads enough to perish one, and the rain too.' The days were not too cold for them, he added, for they were allowed to sit by the fire in the day room. On his second night in custody Warden was permitted what is now known in penal circles as a 'conjugal visit'. James Castleman, who had by then been the town jailer for sixteen years, later said, 'I know that he had a bed, and his wife and child slept with him.'

Although Warden did not appear to suffer from any particular illness, he was certainly not a well man whilst in the jail. Colonel Whitbread himself realised that when he visited him. This is the account he gave to a court about the matter and the resultant moving of the prisoner. 'I observed the man was not well, and I told Mr. Bailey so. In consequence I desired Mr. Short, the surgeon of the regiment, should visit him, or if Mr. Short should think it advisable he should not continue in that species of confinement, he should be removed to his own house; and it was afterwards reported to me that that sort of discretionary order of mine had been executed.' Charles Short was certainly well qualified to make a decision about the prisoner's fitness for close confinement: he was a local surgeon and coroner, and from 1810 to 1844 was to be the visiting medical man at the county jail.[2] It was perhaps this particular incident which, thanks to Whitbread's influence, led to Short's appointment to the county jail post.

Warden's release from the jail took place on Christmas Eve, but thereafter he was kept confined to his own house until shortly before the court-martial. From 26 January until the confirmation of his acquittal on 11 March he was kept in military custody at Yaxley Barracks. Not surprisingly Warden was incensed at his treatment and sought legal advice. As a result of that advice he commenced proceedings for damages for false imprisonment against both

Bailey and Whitbread. However, since he could only recover damages for his loss and suffering once, his action against Bailey proceeded first, whilst that against Whitbread was left in abeyance, to await the outcome of the first trial. The final outcome of that first action against Bailey was not clear until after Whitbread's death in 1815, and we must now examine why there was such a delay.

The action of *Warden v. Bailey* came on first before Mr. Justice Grose and a jury at the Bedford Spring Assizes on Saturday 16 March 1811, a year after Warden's final release. Serjeant Frere led the legal team appearing for the plaintiff, whilst the defendant had two leading counsel, Serjeants Sellon and Peckwell. In his opening speech to the jury on behalf of Warden, Serjeant Frere let himself go, mocking Whitbread and his educational ideas. 'I dare say you recollect perfectly well that Mr. Whitbread once conceived a most general project for educating the whole community. He brought into the House of Commons a Bill for teaching the whole nation in a mass, all the subjects of his Majesty, of all ages and sexes, to read and write, and cast accounts; I dare say he did it with very excellent intentions ...... However, Mr. Whitbread failed in that project. It was thought too visionary for the country. But no sooner was he invested with this authority over his own little kingdom here, his regiment of local militia, than thinking himself absolute among his military subjects, though he had failed in his grand project, yet, where he had the power, he would make the experiment, not at the period of infancy and youth, to occupy himself in the "delightful task of rearing the tender thought, and teaching the young idea how to shoot", but he chose to take forty old, stubborn, hard-fisted sergeants and corporals, local militiamen, and sent them to school in his town of Bedford. I do not know whether there was written over the door

SAMUEL WHITBREAD
AN EVENING SCHOOL

nor can I say whereabout this school was situated. Perhaps at first Schoolmaster Whitbread wished it to be private, that the men might steal down as snugly as possible, to avoid the hooting of the boys in the street; who, you know, would hoot them most tremendously at being sent to this school like grown gentlemen to a London academy, to learn to read and write.'

Doubtless encouraged by smiles and chuckles from the local jury, Serjeant Frere continued, 'The notable part of the scheme was, that this experiment was to be tried at the expense of the subjects, upon whom it was inflicted; and these men, notwithstanding they were to lose their time — a carpenter, whose time by candlelight is as valuable as it is by daylight, is not only subjected to the indignity of going to school in the maturity of life, with all his children laughing at him, but he is to have eightpence a week purloined out of his half-guinea to pay for it; and this, gentlemen, was a job for the sergeant-major, who was to be the teacher and to have the profits. Now I will put the scholarship of Warden against the sergeant-major's, whom I suppose they will call as a witness, if they attempt any justification in this cause. I am told the sergeant-major is a very bad stick as a schoolmaster, and quite incompetent to teach a school. Indeed the whole thing was so exceedingly ridiculous that "Go to school!" was a common cry of the populace wherever any of these men were seen. If one of them found a fault with his own children and threatened to send them to school, he received this answer, "Go to school yourself." '

The lawyer went on to tell the jury of the truancy and imprisoning of his client, and of his later confinement to his own house. He continued, 'But I am informed the usage of the army is for non-commissioned officers to be confined at their quarters. I defy my learned brother to prove that it was necessary to confine this man elsewhere. I defy him to prove that he was refractory — the whole of the case proves to the contrary.' He doubtless enjoyed informing the jury of the outcome of the court-martial. 'The result, gentlemen, was, he was acquitted; the thing was laughed out of court.' Eventually Serjeant Frere got around to calling his witnesses, some of whom have already been quoted. Between them they related the whole of the circumstances surrounding the suffering of the plaintiff.

At the beginning of his opening speech to the jury, Serjeant Sellon, for the defence, took his opponent to task for his jocular manner. 'Gentlemen, I could have wished that my learned friend, in opening this case, had treated it throughout in the way he began to open it, as that case of real solemnity and importance which I feel it to be, which, I am sure, his Lordship and you feel it to be ...... Mr. Whitbread has upon all occasions proved himself to this county a most useful and active magistrate, that he has uniformly been in his political character an assertor of the rights and liberties of the subject, and to this I may add, that he has always, in a remarkable manner distinguished himself as the friend and guardian of the poor.' This tribute was certainly merited.

Counsel went on to take the court through the various parts of military law which he submitted were relevant, including the statutory provision that non-commissioned officers of the local militia were under the command of the adjutant, who was required to obey his colonel's orders. He was at pains to point out that Warden had not been imprisoned for failing to attend school, but for his mutinous words, which required his detention until he could be brought before his commanding officer. Serjeant Sellon next made his most important point: 'It is absolutely out of the power of the courts of common law to take cognizance of any action, the ground of which is the breach of military discipline.' For that proposition he relied on the case of *Sutton v. Johnstone.*[3] The judge intervened to say, 'I cannot distinguish this case from that of *Sutton v. Johnstone.*' Serjeant Frere hastily tried on the plaintiff's behalf to show the judge that the two cases were materially different, but he was unsuccessful. Mr. Justice Grose said that in his view the plaintiff's 'action will not lie', and that Warden should have complained to a military court. Serjeant Frere rightly pointed out that such a court could not award damages, but the judge could not be moved, and he non-suited the plaintiff, without calling on the defendant to produce any evidence.

The plaintiff and his lawyers did not take this defeat lying down, but appealed to the Court of Common Pleas, presided over by the Chief Justice Sir James Mansfield.[4] When Bailey's lawyers were seeking to justify the evening classes on the grounds that sergeants had to be able to write, Mr. Justice Lawrence intervened with some pertinent comments. 'It is no part of the military duty to attend a school and learn to write and read. If writing is necessary to corporals and sergeants, the superior officer must select men who can write and read; and if they do not continue to do it well, they may be reduced to the ranks.' On 28 June 1811 Chief Justice Mansfield delivered the judgment of the court. He pointed out that at Bedford Assizes 'the learned judge was desired to non-suit the plaintiff upon the grounds of a doctrine, supposed to be established by the case of *Sutton v. Johnstone*, that an inferior officer cannot maintain an action against a superior officer for imprisonment inflicted in consequence of disobedience to any command whatever, issued by the superior to the inferior officer. To be sure, that is a very wide inference to draw from *Sutton v. Johnstone*, that being only a case of imprisonment for disobedience to the orders issued in the heat of a battle, where obedience, and instant obedience, is necessary.' The instant case was clearly quite different.

The Chief Justice went on to point out that the order to go to school was probably not justified. 'But with respect to the order itself, it might indeed be very convenient that a military officer might be enabled to make the men under his command learn to read and write, it might be very useful, but it is not a part of military discipline. Then, further, there is a tax of eightpence a week for learning to read and write. Now if the House of Lords had inserted in an act of parliament, that sergeants and corporals should pay eightpence per week for learning to read and write, the bill, on coming down to the Lower House, would certainly have been thrown out; and clearly a commanding officer of a regiment cannot impose that tax. We think then that the order to attend the school most probably was bad, and an excess of authority, but the order of taxation was certainly so; and that order was never rescinded. The subject cannot be taxed, even in the most indirect way, unless it originates in the lower house of parliament.' The authority for the latter proposition was so fundamental that the Chief Justice did not cite it; it was, of course, Magna Carta, and the usages which followed on it. 'We therefore think the rule must be made absolute for a new trial.' He went on to express certain wishes, similar to those which Serjeant Sellon had reported to Whitbread by letter two days earlier.

Sellon, who had accurately gauged the court's views, wrote: 'The inclination of the court certainly appears against the non-suit and in all probability the rule for a new trial will be made absolute. What the result of another trial may be I do not pretend to say — but it has been more than once in the course of the argument strongly recommended by the Chief Justice to put an end to both actions and not to bring to a public decision questions of so delicate a nature as are involved in them — especially at this time when no good consequence could result from it, either to the Army or the country. My Brother Blosset and myself are of opinion that considering all the circumstances it might be advisable to submit the whole case to a private enquiry — we therefore wish to know whether you object to leave both causes to the arbitration of some eminent barrister who should take both the law and the facts into consideration.'[5] (Serjeant Peckwell had changed his name to Blosset after the trial.)

It is not clear what Whitbread's or Bailey's response to the two suggestions were, but it is clear that the disputes were neither settled nor referred to arbitration, for on Saturday 3 August 1811 the case of *Warden v. Bailey* started all over again at Bedford Assizes — and in front of the Chief Justice who had urged the parties to settle it. Serjeant Frere's opening speech on this occasion was much more sober: he did not attempt to repeat his mocking comments. He soon clashed with the Chief Justice on an interesting point. Richard Warden had clearly been in trouble again, after the original court-martial, and before the Summer Assizes, for his name was included as a prisoner in the jail calendar which was placed before the Chief Justice. The calendar showed that he had been committed to the county jail on 26 July 1811 after a regimental court-martial on the two preceding days. His offence on this occasion must have been rather more serious than merely refusing to attend school, for he had been sentenced to two months imprisonment and to be reduced to the ranks.[6] At the opening of the Assizes he was released by proclamation, but when Serjeant Frere referred to this incident in his opening speech to the jury in the re-trial of the civil action, the Chief Justice rebuked him. Frere suggested that there was something sinister about the whole affair, saying to the jury, 'I thought it a very decided and strong attempt to bring into question this right and jurisdiction of military officers to confine in his Majesty's jail.' 'What has that commitment to do with this cause?' the Chief Justice asked. 'It ought not to be mentioned in this cause; it has nothing to do with it.' He went on to accuse the serjeant of attempting to mislead the jury, and thereafter Frere concluded his opening speech within seconds.

Shortly after this Whitbread was advised by the Secretary at War that he had consulted with the Judge Advocate-General and the Attorney General about the effect of Warden's discharge from the county jail.[7] The Secretary continued, 'I am of opinion that you are not to consider the proceeding of the judges of Assize as annulling the sentence of the court-martial altogether, but as affecting only that part of the sentence to which it immediately relates, i.e. the imprisonment in the common jail. That you are therefore to consider Mr. Warden as still in a state of degradation − that you have the power of remitting any part or all of such sentence at your discretion.' Whitbread was also advised that 'neither the Mutiny Act nor the practice of the Service authorise the pointing out the common jail as a place of confinement for military offenders'.[8] The military authorities had perhaps drawn the attention of the Chief Justice to this point before the Assizes. In any event, the duty of the judges to deliver the jail would have led to Warden's release, even without the intervention of the Judge Advocate-General.

After this digression, we must return to the second civil trial. Serjeant Frere called much the same evidence for the plaintiff as on the first occasion to prove his wrongful imprisonment by Bailey. Thereafter the trial took a different course from the first one, for evidence was on this occasion called on behalf of the defendant. Many of the witnesses were senior military officers, including General Pigot himself, partly called to prove that Whitbread had not delayed in bringing Warden before the first court-martial. However, Whitbread himself gave evidence designed to show that even if Bailey had been responsible for the imprisonment of the plaintiff for the first two days of his time in the town jail, thereafter the responsibility had been his alone. He said that when Warden was brought before him on Monday 4 December 1809 and he had heard the charges made against him, 'I ordered Sergeant Richard Warden to be taken back to prison. That was my order and my order only, delivered to the adjutant for him to execute, on my account.' He was also asked about the regimental guard room, a former comb shop which William Stapleton had let to the adjutant, and which the plaintiff's counsel were suggesting would have been a more suitable place for a military prisoner. 'It is a very improper place, in my opinion', replied Whitbread, 'to confine a man for three weeks at any period of the year, much less in the winter.'

Amongst the other witnesses for the defence was Sergeant-Major Warner, but during his evidence the Chief Justice displayed the impatience he had shown earlier in the case, 'That does not signify a farthing,' said his Lordship, when questions were being asked of Warner about Warden's ability to write. At the end of the witness's testimony he snorted, 'This really does not at all signify; it is wasting time.' Sergeant Thomas Smith was the principal witness to give evidence about Warden's alleged mutinous words directed at Cooper, and he was not shaken in cross-examination, during which he revealed that he was an auctioneer's clerk, adding, 'Sometimes I buy a few pigs.'

James Castleman, the town jailer, gave evidence to prove that Warden's imprisonment had not been all that hard for him to bear. He almost described his little jail in the glowing terms of the modern estate agent trying to sell a property. He also cheerfully admitted that he had held Warden without any written authority whatsoever, and that he had often obliged other regiments similarly 'only by verbal direction of the commanding officer'. General Pigot also gave evidence about the use of civilian prisons by the Army, and this prompted the Chief Justice to comment: 'I have no doubt, where they have no other prisons, they have taken the liberty to send to the jail; but it is a curious custody, because the jailer may let him out whenever he pleases.'

After the conclusion of the evidence the Chief Justice summed up the case to the jury fairly briefly. He immediately disposed of the suggestion that the plaintiff's imprisonment after the first two days was not the responsibility of the adjutant. He pointed out that the law does not permit one to rely on an illegal order given by a superior officer — a point made with considerable emphasis at the Nuremberg War Crimes Trials. He told the jury, 'If a colonel issues an illegal order to an adjutant, if that adjutant furthers that order and carries it into execution, the order of his superior officer will not defend him; he must see that the act is legal.'

Having directed the jury that Bailey was responsible for the imprisonment of Warden from beginning to end, he turned to the question of the legality of the order to attend school. Not surprisingly, the Chief Justice repeated the views he had expressed on the application for the new trial. 'That order, I must tell you, appears to me certainly not warranted by law. You have heard that the same thing has been done in other regiments: I dare say it has ...... I do not know that there is any law by which they could be compelled to go at a stated time every evening to improve themselves in reading and writing.' He told the jury that they had to decide whether Warden had spoken the words to Cooper at all, and cautioned them, 'But you will consider whether the words here can, in any fair sense put upon the words "mutiny" and "sedition", be here said to be mutinous and seditious.'

In all the circumstances it was not surprising that the jury returned a verdict in favour of the plaintiff, awarding him £100 damages, together with a further £34 to compensate him for the expense of his defence at the first court-martial at which he had been acquitted. The successful plaintiff did not stay in Bedford for long. He had obviously had enough of the local militia and decided to join the regular army at Canterbury. On 20 January 1812 Bailey wrote to Whitbread, 'Sergeant Barringer states that Richard Warden has enlisted in the 3rd. Dragoons — if so he will stand a chance of getting his deserts.'[9] Whitbread now behaved in an extraordinarily vindictive manner.

Instead of merely writing back to Bailey, 'Thank goodness we are rid of him', he wrote to claim Warden back, as he had not asked the permission of his colonel to enlist in the army! On 20 February Major R. Gossip of the 3rd. King's Own Dragoons wrote to confirm that Warden had indeed enlisted in his unit six weeks earlier. He added, 'With every disposition to accede to your prior, and it would seem well-founded claim to the man — yet, as the circumstances appear to be of no ordinary nature, I trust you will consider I am not doing more than my duty in submitting the case for the consideration and opinion of the Right Honble. The Secretary at War.'[10] On 15 April Major Gossip wrote to say that he had heard from the Secretary, 'And I am commanded to request you will be pleased to favour me with the man's discharge from the former corps'.[11] Thereafter Whitbread seems to have been content to let Warden go his own way, but where that way led one cannot say.

It may well have been Whitbread's intransigence which led to the rumour that he had had men flogged in his unit. On 27 March the printer of the *Beacon* wrote to him from London: 'I beg to inform you that a letter has been sent for insertion, and which will appear on Sunday next, stating that though you have so nobly advocated the cause of humanity respecting military flogging, yet that you have suffered such practice to prevail in your own regiment. Sir, we do not believe the rumour, which we consider to have originated from a malevolent party to hurt you at the General Election. As our paper is in great circulation in the neighbourhood of Bedford, we hope you will oblige us with a few lines to put to silence your calumniators, our columns being at all times open to you.'[12]

Whitbread answered indignantly on 31 March. 'You may give the most flat contradiction to your correspondent, who is entirely misinformed, if not worse. Not a strike or a blow has been inflicted upon any one man of the Bedfordshire Local Militia, which I have the honour to command from the time of its being first embodied down to the present moment, and I trust there never will.'[13] He went on to recount the fact that one man in the past had been sentenced by a court-martial to be flogged, but that he was pardoned by his second-in-command, Lord Tavistock, at the very last minute, 'at the halberts'.

Whitbread was very dissatisfied with the result of the second trial and persuaded Bailey to appeal. Although at the trial he had said on oath, 'I am under no obligation whatever to pay the costs of this action', he clearly was footing the bills. On 8 September 1811 Joseph Eade, the attorney of Hitchin, asked him for £400 in respect of legal costs. Whitbread paid half at once, and the balance in the following May.[14] He also decided that the proceedings should be published, and suggested as much to the shorthand writer, W.B. Gurney. The latter replied on 17 August 1811, 'I feel very much obliged by the offer but doubt the sale being sufficient to answer the expense.'[15] In the event, the book of the trial was put out some months later by James Ridgway, of Piccadilly, London, a radical publisher used by some of Whitbread's Whig friends, particularly Henry Brougham. In the preface to *The Trial of an Action for False Imprisonment* Whitbread explained, 'The interest excited by this case, and the importance to the Army of the questions raised in the cause ...... have induced Mr. Whitbread to publish, for general information, the proceedings which have hitherto taken place; and have led to a determination to bring the case before a court of error. To that end a bill of exceptions, to the directions of the Chief Justice to the Jury, was tendered and allowed by his Lordship, and will be argued as early as the legal forms will admit of its being brought on.'

Bailey's lawyers had considerable difficulty in getting the appeal under way. On 1 November 1811 Whitbread was advised by his attorney, 'I have seen Sellon and Blosset. They are apprehensive, particularly Sellon, that Mansfield will try to suppress the question by refusing the bill of exceptions; this would I believe be to do what no judge ever did before. I have strongly urged your expectation, and the general expectation. Sellon has engaged to go tomorrow with Blosset to Mansfield to claim his signature.'[16] When Warden's leading counsel, Serjeant Frere, saw the draft bill of exceptions, he took exception to it, and suggested that the best course, in view of the dispute between the parties about some of the submissions at the trial, was to 'apply at once to Mr. Cox, the Chief Justice's marshall, for his notes, which must be referred to in the last resort.'[17] Sir Arthur Pigott, who had been the Whig Attorney-General in the Administration of All the Talents, in which Whitbread had failed to get a post, was retained to lead on Bailey's behalf on the hearing of the appeal.

For some reason, which does not emerge from the Whitbread documents, Bailey's appeal did not come on for hearing until the Easter term in 1815.[18] The judgment of the court was not delivered by Lord Ellenborough, Chief Justice of the King's Bench, until 23 November 1815, too late for Whitbread to hear, for he had committed suicide on 5 July. He would have been disappointed by the result, for Bailey's appeal was dismissed. And so ended a very unfortunate series of storms in one small teacup.

No more was heard of Warden, but Bailey, who as Whitbread's agent had prepared very careful lists showing all voters, as well as other information,[19] was Mayor of Bedford in 1827 and 1831. The schoolmaster, Sergeant Major Warner, also had an interesting career. On 12 September 1813 he wrote to Bailey: 'I should esteem it a favour if you will be kind enough to return Colonel Whitbread my sincere thanks for his kindness in releasing me from my late permanent situation, as also for the numerous favours he has conferred upon me during the time I have been serving under him, and to express my readiness at any time to render my assistance to the regiment that lies in my power. I some time since mentioned to you the benefit I thought a small piece of land would be to me, and you were kind enough to say you would bear it in mind; your interest in that respect with Colonel Whitbread will very much oblige.'[20] Bailey passed the letter on to his colonel, and it was doubtless as a result of Whitbread's intercession that Thomas Warner became the jailer of the county jail in 1814. For twenty years thereafter Warner was the jailer, under the watchful eyes of the principal visiting justice, the Reverend Philip Hunt, Rector of St. Peter's.[21]

1. The source of all information in this article, unless otherwise stated, is *The Trial of an Action for False Imprisonment Brought by Sergeant Richard Warden against Lieutenant and Adjutant Bailey,* 1811, a copy of which is in the Bedfordshire County Library, Reference Library.
2. See, Eric Stockdale, 'A Study of Bedford Prison 1660-1877', Vol. 56 *B.H.R.S.,* 1977, p. 166.
3. *Durnford and East's Reports,* Vol. 1, p. 493.
4. *Warden v. Bailey, English Reports,* Vol. 128, p. 253.
5. *Beds C.R.O.* W 1/473. The Whitbread correspondence is quoted by kind permission of Samuel Charles Whitbread Esq.
6. W 1/479.
7. W 1/476.
8. W 1/477.
9. W 1/490/1.
10. W 1/493.
11. W 1/500.
12. W 1/498.
13. W 1/499.
14. W 1/480, 481 and 509.
15. W 1/516.
16. W 1/487/1.
17. W 1/492.
18. *Bailey v. Warden, English Reports,* Vol. 105, p. 882.
19. Z 231/1 and 2.
20. W 1/526.
21. For Philip Hunt, see p. 31, *supra;* for Hunt and Warner's collaboration see, Eric Stockdale, *op. cit.* chapters 7 and 8.

V
THE COMING OF THE POLICE

For centuries the principal local citizen concerned with the maintenance of law and order, other than the justice of the peace, was the constable. He was an ordinary citizen appointed to serve for one year only, and he was expected to keep himself and his business going as usual. It could be a dangerous task.[1] He was all on his own, unless he could persuade his fellow citizens to come to his aid — something they were bound to do in certain circumstances. Michael Dalton in 1677 put it as follows: 'Every of these conservators of the peace are by the ancient Common Law to imploy their own valour, and may also command the meet help, aid and force of others, to arrest and pacifie all such who in their presence and within their jurisdiction and limits, by word or deed, shall go about to break the peace.'[2]

Over the years it became increasingly clear to magistrates and others in the county that the task of maintaining the peace and of apprehending offenders could not be left to the constables alone — no matter how willing they might be, and some were clearly less willing than others. Various methods were adopted to supplement the limited powers and abilities of the constable.

It has always been the right of the citizen to defend himself, and there is nothing wrong in the idea of proper collective self-defence. We have seen how during the 1757 militia riots, when the constables were understandably keeping a low profile, Lord Royston, Thomas Potter and others were joining in an association to keep the peace. Similarly, throughout the country associations were set up for the apprehension of felons. Adrian Shubert has found 'there were at least 450 associations created in England and Wales between 1744 and 1856'.[3] As Joyce Godber has pointed out, the Olney, Turvey and Harrold Association was founded in 1796, and that of Hockliffe, Chalgrave, Battlesden and Tilsworth four years later.[4] The felons apprehended had often committed minor thefts of food from shops or gardens. As we have seen, Philip Hunt in 1827 gave a Parliamentary Select Committee his views about one of the effects of the existence of such associations. He clearly thought that it was the provision of liberal expenses by the associations to the pursuers of minor offenders which might have been partially responsible for the increase in the number of convictions in the county.

On some occasions when the constable was not able to cope assistance was summoned from the capital, for London had such extensive crime problems that it was ahead of the rest of the country with its development of the police. In 1748 Henry Fielding became a justice of the peace for Westminster, thanks to his 'great patron', the Duke of Bedford, who was also the landlord of the Bow Street courthouse. According to Fielding, the Duke persuaded him that the office would be a very lucrative one.[5] As is well-known, the Bow Street runners formed an early police force with some detection skills, and in 1809 they were called in to help the constable of Ampthill solve a double murder.

On 20 January James Crick, a dairyman, and his widowed housekeeper, Rebecca Read, were found savagely murdered at Lidlington. The Ampthill constable, John Kingston, shortly afterwards presented a bill to quarter sessions for £8.19.10, 'relating to the apprehending and keeping in custody of — Lane, who was charged on suspicion of being concerned in the murder of James Crick and his housekeeper at Lidlington'.[6] Unfortunately the constable had arrested the wrong man, and he was duly released. Sadly, the Bow Street runners were no more successful, though they displayed a great deal of ability to dash about, and to consume ale. They also organised the printing of five hundred posters about the terrible crime. One of the runners sent a detailed bill from the Public Office in Bow Street:

'Jan 24 1809: Pearks going to Woburn, Lidlington and Ampthill and making enquiries respecting the murder of Mr. Crick and his housekeeper	4. 4.0
Coach from London to Woburn	16.0
Coachman and guard	3.0
Chaise from Woburn to Lidlington and Ampthill	13.6
Boy and gates	3.0
Coach from Ampthill to London	16.0
Four days expenses	2.16.0
	£9.13.6

One can guess what some of the expenses were incurred for from the bill submitted by one of the Pearks' colleagues, which included 'Five dinners 7/6; Ale 12/6d.'[7] The murderer was never detected, although according to a later governor of Bedford prison, Robert Evan Roberts, 'In 1836 a man named Kingston, a butcher, about two weeks before his death, made a confession of the murder'.[8] If this report by the governor was true, then it may not have been a coincidence that the name of the constable who made an early arrest of the wrong man, and the name of the man confessing to the crime, was Kingston in each case. In fairness to the constable it should be added that there appears to be no evidence of the confession other than that contained in the governor's note, and that whilst the date of the confession was said to be 1836, Roberts did not arrive at the prison to take over until 1853. Roberts may have got his information from one of the prison records or from another document, but he did not state the source of his information.

In his account of the rural unrest shortly before and during 1830 Alan Cirket has given an amusing example of another occasion when law enforcement seemed to call for a rather excessive expenditure on ale, even though the Bow Street runners were not involved. After some serious poaching incidents at the end of 1829, one of the Duke of Bedford's gamekeepers had suggested that the runners should be sent for once again. The Duke, perhaps recalling their lack of success at Lidlington in 1809, was against the idea, as he thought the runners were 'useless out of London, and a good active and intelligent constable at Bedford or in the neighbourhood of Wootton and Kempston will be much more efficient'. Cirket suggested that some of the constables took advantage of the confidence the Duke reposed in them, by imbibing rather freely. The High Constable of Redbornstoke hundred employed several constables and other assistants and presented the Duke's London Steward with a bill for £111 odd. The Steward complained that in the bill for the *Flying Horse* at Lidlington '93 pots of ale are charged for 10 prisoners and 12 keepers for supper and breakfast ...... The Ampthill bill is worse.'[9] Cirket also showed that special constables were extensively recruited during the 1830 riots, Thomas Potter Macqueen of Ridgmont alone putting in a claim for two shillings a man to be paid for each of the sixty-three specials of his parish.

The Metropolitan Police Act was passed in 1829 and since that time the capital has been policed by the professional force which was then set up. Lidlington having been the scene of the crime which led to the Bow Street runners being called in in 1809, it was trouble at Lidlington which led to the Metropolitan Police being asked for help in 1835. On 11 May the new relieving officer appointed under the new, and very unpopular, poor law, came to Lidlington and was met by a mob which presented him with two unpalatable alternatives: his 'blood or money' was demanded. The trouble spread, particularly to Ampthill, and a number of special constables were sworn in under the provisions of the Special Constables Act of 1831. A further eleven men refused to be sworn in and were duly fined. The Assistant Poor Law Commissioner was sent off to London to ask for government help and the Metropolitan Police were ordered to provide assistance. An Inspector and twenty men arrived and, in the best traditions of the force, stood for no nonsense. They arrested a number of suspects and the trouble died down, leaving the officers free to return to the city. As a precaution, four troops of Yeomanry were called out and moved to Luton, but they played no part in the restoration of order at Ampthill.[10] Incidentally, the Yeomanry and other military bodies in Bedfordshire, were never tempted to copy the appalling conduct of their colleagues at St. Peter's Field in Manchester in 1819: there is no record of any serious misuse of military power in the county.

In 1832 Sir Robert Peel, the father of the Metropolitan Police, tried to persuade the Whig government, which included Lord John Russell, to provide for police forces for towns other than London, but at that time he was unsuccessful. As T.A. Critchley, the historian of the police, has pointed out, in 1833 'Parliament enacted a stop-gap measure, the Lighting and Watching Act, which was the first statute to deal with the establishment of paid police forces in the country generally'.[11] Luton was one of the first towns to take advantage of this stop-gap measure. In 1835 the Municipal Corporations Act was passed and amongst other major changes it provided for the boroughs with charters to set up their own police forces if they wished, and the Bedford Corporation in that year decided that the time had come for the town to have its own constabulary. That left only the counties without any statutory provision for setting up their own forces.

Back in 1821 one of the better Bedford constables, John Hopkins Warden, had made some very sensible suggestions to quarter sessions. 'The extent of crime regularly committed in this county, and the organised bands which perpetrate robbery of almost every description, require an active police for many reasons. First, that a general knowledge may be obtained of loose and desperate characters in this county, which can only be obtained by persons whose business it is to search them out. Second, it can only be by practice that the officer becomes acquainted with the artful devices of experienced robbers, their modes of communication with each other, their system of plunder, and the disposal of their booty. The inexperienced constable, who is perhaps new to his office every year, cannot be aware of their manoeuvres; in short, he has other objects in view. His business of all things must be attended and knowing that his term of service will soon expire, he cannot, *he does not* give it the attention his office and country require. But the experienced officer strikes at once to the point. His first clue serves him as the sea mark and past cases instruct his proceedings; the old offender will find his old devices fail and the juvenile depredator will be deterred from crime by speedy exposure ...... If the magistracy of this or any county wish to see an active police who will do their duty, it must be made a business of the officer, or officers must have a something as a dependance, for no man of business can indefinitely do his duty if he becomes an object of attack, he is called sly, meddlesome and a troublesome man; the lower classes in life attack him with every opprobrious name in the society they move, and every endeavour is made by them to injure him in his profession.'[12]

Warden clearly had the right idea, but on one occasion he allowed his enthusiasm to get the better of him. In 1826 he appeared before quarter sessions as he had wrongly, whilst constable, described himself as 'Inspector of Weights and Measures', going so far as to mark and alter certain weights. He admitted to the court that he had received over £30 for his unauthorised services. The court declared firmly that only Messrs. Kilpin of Bedford were entitled to act as Inspectors.[13]

Rather more important than Warden's contribution to the debate on the desirability of a regular police force for the county, was that of Lord John Russell, the Home Secretary in 1839. On 24 July he moved in the House of Commons for leave to bring in a bill for establishing county and district constabularies. He proposed by the bill to give authority to the justices to set up a local force. He pointed out that the existing provisions relating to special constalbes were no adequate substitute. According to *Hansard* Lord John Russell said that 'It certainly was in the power of justices to add to the number of special constables on any sudden necessity; but whenever that extended beyond a certain point they found themselves very much at a loss. Many evils had arisen from that: and it was very frequently the case, that when apprehensions arose with respect to any meeting about to be held, the magistrates sent directly for military assistance. The officers commanding in the districts to which such applications were made felt them to be very embarrassing ...... Applications of that kind tended to break and destroy the discipline of the troops ...... It was very obvious that on many occasions this necessity would be prevented if there existed a civil force of constabulary which could be relied on by the magistrates. The military, though they were able to put down disorder, were useless in capturing and arresting the persons who had caused it.'[14]

Warden had been concerned about the need for police officers to deal with ordinary criminal offences; the Home Secretary was more concerned about civil disorder. He was aware of what had been happening in the country, and especially in his home county. Although fears had been expressed at different times by Members of Parliament and others about the dangers inherent in a police force such as the French had, the concern about disorder in the country was enough for the County Police Act to be passed.

The justices at Bedfordshire quarter sessions at once began to discuss the setting up of a county force. A committee recommended that a chief constable should be appointed at a yearly salary of £250, together with six superintendents at £75, and twenty constables at a weekly sum of ten shillings. The recommendations were accepted on 28 January 1840, save that the justices decided to double the number of the constables to forty. Captain Edward Moore Boultbee was appointed to head the new force, and his residence was required to be at Ampthill.[15]

The justices made some interesting comments on the earlier arrangements. 'The inefficiency of the present system will readily be admitted on all sides and may perhaps be traced to the following causes:

1. The inadequate payment of parish constables, and the consequent unwillingness of persons the best qualified to undertake the office.

2. That their duties are not clearly defined.

3. That there is no co-operation or communication between the constables of different parishes.

4. That they are not in any way organised under the Chief Constable or otherwise for active and efficient service.

The Chief Constables in the present day are seldom if ever occupied in preserving or restoring the peace, in the apprehension of offenders or in the prevention of crime and if at any time they are, are not remunerated for it. It may also be admitted that in many parts of the country, with the increase of trade and manufactures and the increase of population there is also an alarming increase in crime. This does not appear to be the case in Bedfordshire, which may be attributed to the absence of manufacturers, the improved state of agriculture and a diminution of game preserves, at least to the extent to which they were carried on some years ago.'[16]

The last sentiments were perhaps unjustified, and may be compared with the similar degree of smugness shown by the Mayor of Bedford when he replied to the county's offer of a joint force. On 16 January 1840 Theed Pearse, the Clerk of the Peace, wrote to Thomas Abbott Green, the Mayor of the borough, which had already taken advantage of the 1835 Act to set up its own force. Pearse informed the Mayor, 'The Town of Bedford is omitted, the Committee doubting whether they are authorised by the Act to include it, but I am directed to inform you that if the Town should desire to be included, if upon application to the Secretary of State they should learn they are authorised to include them, they will be ready to do so.'[17] On the following day the Town Clerk sent out a notice to his councillors summoning them to a meeting on 21 January 'to take into consideration the expedience of uniting the Borough Police or any branch thereof with the Police of the County proposed to be established'.

The Town Council clearly felt rather superior, as the Mayor's answer to Pearse on 21 January indicated. 'The Town Council beg respectfully to decline the union, and they do so because they consider the proposed force is totally inadequate to perform the various and important services contemplated by the Act.' The Mayor pointed out that most serious crimes were committed at night, adding, 'At the various quarter sessions and assizes the number of prisoners from the Town of Bedford for trial, happily, bear a very insignificant proportion to the number of inhabitants which now exceeds 9000, which absence the Town Council mainly attribute to the system of watching introduced into the Town and which has during the present winter prevented robbery of any kind whatever during the hours of darkness.'

As a result of this brush off the county and borough police forces remained separate for more than a century, ultimately merging in 1947.[18]

The justices had no sooner decided to set up a constabulary than the offers from tailoring firms came in, offering the finest uniforms for the new force. A letter from Charles Hebbert and Company, of Pall Mall East in London, dated 26 February 1840, read as follows: 'Not being sure whether Mr. Pearse is at this time Clerk of the Peace I address my letter to the officer rather than the individual. If it be still Mr. Pearse he will remember me as nephew of the late Dr. Hunt and having occasionally met him at Bedford and I think at my brother's, the Rev. Joseph Gould's. I am now a partner in the Army and Police Clothing establishment of Charles Hebbert and Company and desirous of adding the Bedfordshire Police to our list. We have clothed the Metropolitan Police (now 4000 men) since its commencement entirely to the satisfaction of the Commissioners and the comfort, uniformity and efficiency of the men.' The letter was signed Nathaniel Gould.[19] On 11 March the Clerk of the Peace informed Gould and his partners that they had succeeded in getting the contract to equip the new force. Whilst Philip Hunt's name must still have been greatly respected in Bedford two years after his death, it was probably the mention of the Metropolitan Police orders which secured Gould his contract, rather than the use of his uncle's name, or any form of post-mortem nepotism.

The county force was now ready for its first recruits: and a very unpromising lot they were. The first record book shows that nine men in turn were known as P.C.1 in the first ten years of the constabulary.[20] Lest it be thought that the burden of bearing the number 1 was too much for the average man, and that it contributed to the departure of eight P.C.1's, the reader may care to see the entries relating to the first officers bearing the initial sixteen numbers.

'No. 1, Frederick Porter, joined 25 March 1840. 18 July 1840, suspended for being drunk on duty. Reinstated with a caution: to be discharged for the next offence. 7 October 1840, dismissed the force for general bad conduct.

No. 2, Charles Price, joined 25 March 1840. 22 February 1843, resigned.

No. 3, Samuel Allin, joined 19 April 1840. 10 February 1841, resigned.

No. 4, James Cooper, joined 6 April 1840. 29 July 1840, allowed to resign, there being doubts as to his honesty in money matters.

No. 5, Joseph Shaw, joined 6 May 1840. 24 March 1841, resigned.

No. 6, Samuel Owen, joined 22 April 1840. 7 July 1840, fined 10/- for disobeying orders for wearing his private clothes while on duty, and visiting another division without permission. 28 July 1840, ordered to be discharged on 5 August, he being unfit for the situation of police constable.

No. 7, Daniel Herbert, joined 25 March 1840. 17 March 1841, resigned.

No. 8, Daniel Hazard, joined 25 March 1840.

No. 9, Edward Scott, joined 25 March 1840. 16 June 1847, fined 20/- for making a false report while doing duty in the Bletsoe division.

No. 10, Francis Roberts, joined 28 March 1840. 24 March 1841, resigned.

No. 11, George Lacy, joined 14 April 1840. 19 August 1840, dismissed the force for general bad conduct.

No. 12, Thomas Vear, joined 27 March 1840. 22 July 1840, fined 10/- for neglect of duty while attending the feast at Cranfield on 6 July 1840. 29 April 1842, fined 20/- for allowing William Roberts, a prisoner, to escape out of custody. 25 December 1844, dismissed.

No. 13, Henry Gamble, joined 6 April 1840. 9 July 1840, reprimanded by Capt. Boultbee for being drunk on duty. 16 March 1842, resigned.

No. 14, William Breakwell, joined 6 April 1840. 23 April 1840, fined 10/- for playing cricket and drinking in a public house when ordered on duty at Potton fair the 20th. instant. 27 October 1847, Biggleswade Bench, P.C. Breakwell charged on summons by William Daniels, Girtford, with assaulting him on 12th. instant; settled out of court by Breakwell paying 20/- for loss of time and 5/- for doctor's bill.

No. 15, John Geary, joined 8 April 1840. 23 April 1840, fined 10/- for playing cricket and drinking in a public house when ordered on duty at Potton fair the 20th. instant. 23 June 1840, fined 10/- for leaving his beat at 12.30 a.m. without permission from his superintendent. 25 February 1841, resigned.

No. 16, Thomas Davies, joined 7 April 1840. 6 May 1840, dismissed for being drunk on duty.'

It should be added that the force settled down after a while, having no doubt refined its selection procedures. Furthermore, the process of maturation helped some of the younger officers to turn into responsible men. For example, P.C.9, Edward Scott, served successfully for a further nineteen years after his slight lapse in 1847.

The reaction of the public to the new county police was mixed. Some citizens approved of the new force, and their only complaint was that there were not enough men in it to cope with all the criminals in their particular area. Others thought that the force was unnecessary, and that it should be abolished. Their motives for opposition were probably mixed, but one can detect in many of the petitions and memorials a certain pre-occupation with the expense involved. Ratepayers, by and large, seem to have objected to the increases they were being asked to pay — something their descendants would not dream of doing! Some towns sent in two petitions to quarter sessions: one asking for more police, the other for less.[21]

Some citizens of Leighton Buzzard sent in a memorial dated 25 August 1840 showing: 'That the town of Leighton Buzzard contains a population of 5000 or thereabouts. That a large market is held there weekly and seven fairs in the course of the year. That the inns and houses licensed for the sale of beer are very numerous. That owing to the establishment of the Leighton Station on the London and Birmingham Railway the thoroughfare is considerable and daily increasing. That sheepstealing and depredations on gardens and on houses has increased to an alarming extent. That the present police (two in number) are utterly insufficient to protect property or maintain good order in the streets. That your memorialists are of opinion that the police force ought to be increased as soon as possible.'

Other residents of Leighton Buzzard, who had met on 26 July, sent in a petition dated 10 October 1840 calling for the discontinuance of the police, 'considering as we do that the peace and good order of our locality render the vast expense of a rural police an useless expenditure of our money'.

The residents of Luton were similarly divided. Their first memorial is interesting because it shows how Luton was developing and how the town had made use of the Lighting and Watching Act of 1833. 'We, the undersigned Inspectors of Lighting and Watching the township of Luton, acting under the provisions of an Act of Parliament, 3 & 4 William IV, beg respectfully to report to your worships that we conceive the number of constables of the Bedfordshire rural police force stationed at Luton to be inadequate to the due performance of the duties required of them in this neighbourhood. We beg to submit for your consideration that the *parish* of Luton alone contains nearly 17,000 acres of land with a population of about 7000. That up to the period of the appointment of the rural police force your memorialists employed a day constable and two night watchmen for the protection of the *township* of Luton only, which we found to be scarcely sufficient for the purpose, but upon the establishment of the rural police your memorialists were compelled to discharge their officers, the Act of Parliament depriving them of the means of raising the necessary funds for their support, and your memorialists now find the whole of the parish of Luton placed under the protection of a less number of constables than your memorialists found to be barely sufficient for the duties of the township alone. And your memorialists humbly submit that the present force is far from adequate to the protection of the vast property contained in the warehouses and other buildings in the town of Luton, more especially as regards the duties of the night watch, when such property must necessarily be left in a great measure totally unprotected from fire and robbery. And last your memorialists beg to submit that it is very essential for the proper execution of the duties of a superintendent of police over so large a district, that such officer should have the means of a speedy communication with his subordinates, for which purpose they humbly suggest that he should be provided with a horse.'

Many other residents of Luton were reluctant to pay for police officers, never mind such reckless extravagance as a horse. Together with others living in different areas, they put their names to a printed petition which included the following polite, and possibly undeserved, reference to the existing officers. 'Your petitioners have watched very attentively the working of the present system, and your petitioners are of opinion that a rural police establishment in this county must necessarily be expensive, if not inefficient. That your petitioners, while they disclaim any intention of casting the slightest reflection upon the persons composing that force, do not believe that they receive a benefit at all corresponding with the enormous expense incurred.'

One of the signatories of the Houghton Regis petition entreating the justices 'to take into your serious consideration the propriety of relieving us altogether from the recent police force in this parish', was so carried away that he added: 'I am that I am weary of the police'.

The inhabitants of Woburn Sands stated 'that the want of a policeman resident in the village is urgently felt by your petitioners', and they made a useful suggestion about co-operation with the adjoining county. 'Your petitioners therefore pray that, either alone or in conjunction with the police authorities of the county of Bucks, in which a portion of the district is situated, you would cause a policeman to be regularly situated in Woburn Sands.' Unfortunately, the records show that one attempt at co-operation between the two county forces failed. The constables' record book already referred to told the sad story. 'P.C. William Champkins, reported for tossing for beer with P.C. 87 Barrett (a Bucks P.C.) in a public house at Leighton, afterwards quarrelling in the street with him and coming to blows. Suspended till 19th. instant by the Chief Constable, then reinstated and fined one week's pay (19/-).'[22]

Fortunately, the petitions calling for the abolition of the force did not succeed, so since 1840 the county has had its own constabulary to keep the peace.

1.   Eric Stockdale, 'The Lot of the Seventeenth Century Constable', *Bedfordshire Magazine,* Vol. 13 (1972), p.256.
2.   Michael Dalton, *The Countrey Justice,* London, 1677, p.5.
3.   Adrian Shubert, 'Private Initiative in Law Enforcement', in Victor Bailey (ed.) *Policing and Punishment in Nineteenth Century Britain,* London: Croom Helm, 1981, p.27.
4.   Joyce Godber, *History of Bedfordshire 1066-1888,* Beds. C.C., 1969, p.407.
5.   Leon Radzinowicz, *A History of English Criminal Law,* London: Stevens, 1956, Vol. 3, p.33.
6.   QSR 1809/110.
7.   QSR 1809/107, 115, 118, 118a.
8.   QSS 4, entry for 1809.
9.   Alan F. Cirket, 'The 1830 Riots in Bedfordshire', *B.H.R.S.* Vol. 57, (1978), p.82, 101.
10.   CRT 150/11, 12.
11.   T.A. Critchley, *A History of Police in England and Wales 900-1966,* London: Constable, 1967, p.60.
12.   QSR 1821/711.
13.   QSM 28/282.